PILGRIMAGES, SANCTUARIES, ICONS, APPARITIONS

An Historical and Scriptural Account

By

Fr. René Laurentin

Translated from French by:

Bro. William Fackovec, S.M.
Int'l Marian Research Institute

Edited and published by:

The Riehle Foundation
P.O. Box 7
Milford, OH 45150

The original manuscript comprises the text for the course, "Pilgrimages, Sanctuaries, Icons and Apparitions;" taught by the author at the Int'l Marian Research Institute, Dayton, Ohio, July, 1994.

Published by: The Riehle Foundation
P.O. Box 7
Milford, OH 45150
513-576-0032

For additional copies contact the publisher.

Additional copies for bookstores and book distributors, contact:

Faith Publishing Company
P.O. Box 237
Milford, OH 45150
513-576-6400

ISBN: 1-877678-30-9

Library of Congress Catalog No.: 94-061409

CONTENTS

Introduction

Throughout the ages, certain aspects of the religious experience have remained constant. This is particularly true in the Catholic Church whose roots go back to the Ascension of Jesus and the early thrusts of evangelization by the Apostles.

In some cases these specific aspects of the experience go back far beyond the coming of the Messiah and are evident in the books of the Old Testament. Such is the case with pilgrimages, sanctuaries, icons, and apparitions.

Most often these four phenomena are associated with the Blessed Virgin Mary, particularly in our current age. However, their existence, and their importance go much deeper and can be found in the earliest civilizations as foundations of mankind's search for God.

Fr. René Laurentin, noted Marian theologian and author of over 100 books, provides some interesting facts and insights concerning pilgrimages, sanctuaries, icons and apparitions. He traces the history back to the earliest times. It is interesting to note the consistency, the permanence of these aspects of the faith down through so many centuries. More importantly, Fr. Laurentin is able to link these four topics to specific passages in the Bible. The Old and New Testaments are thus further linked together through these tangible components and signs used by Christians over so many centuries.

Of course, the first apparition can be traced all the way back to the first few pages of the Bible. Adam and Eve were the recipients. But it didn't take long for Abraham and his descendants to initiate the first appearance of these other hallmarks of our faith and belief in God.

Pilgrimage and sanctuary (shrine) are particularly apparent. Long journeys to specific places of prayer and/or adoration were common. In fact they were just as common in the pagan countries, albeit the wrong gods were being worshipped in contrast. The great pyramids and edifices of the early Egyptians give evidence to it.

What importance do these four phenomena play in our faith, and what meaning do they convey? Is there too much emphasis placed on these types of aspects of our beliefs? Is there anything of idolatry connected with them?

If so, it would appear that Jesus and Mary were guilty. Pilgrimage was a major part of their lives, and so were temples. Jesus went there often. Icons were also part of their religious identities, and Mary was the recipient of apparitions.

We believe this book gives evidence to the fact that we can all use as much help as we can muster up on our own pilgrimage—the one that leads us ultimately to our Creator. Perhaps these four topics can be beneficial as aids and stimulants to your faith, and also to your knowledge of their origin.

The Riehle Foundation

PART I

CHAPTER 1

Pilgrimages, Shrines, Icons, Apparitions

Pilgrimages and shrines, icons and apparitions, are four visible aspects of Christian cult. They are interconnected. People make pilgrimages to shrines, where they venerate icons; and the most important of them have been established at places of apparitions.

But these aspects are very different from each other. Pilgrimages are rather dynamic while shrines and icons are static objects. Apparitions are exceptional events and a work of God. The first three, on the contrary are a human work. Apparitions are formally of supernatural origin when they are authentic; hence the importance of discernment in this matter.

Pilgrimages are a human endeavor: a bodily movement, a physical going forth that engages body and soul. A shrine, on the other hand, is a stable place: its prestige and its attraction are linked to its immovable permanence. It is often a building, where at times pilgrims spend the night, stretched out in the midst of their baggage, as at Fatima, where the shrine's collonades are extended like arms to welcome them.

The icon, on the contrary, is a picture of two dimensions: a humble colored surface that becomes a window opening on to Heaven. It is an image made by the hand

1

of man. An apparition, on the other hand, is a gift from Heaven, an immediate perception of the invisible, communicated to the seers in a way that is strictly gratuitous and personal. But its objectivity is not easily demonstrable (as contrasted with a temple or an icon, which can be verified in all kinds of ways).

The Shroud of Turin is somewhere between icons and apparitions: earthly as is an icon, but like an apparition, "not made by the hand of man." It is the imprint of the body of Christ, but a material imprint and no doubt natural, although no complete explanation for it has been found. Furthermore, an icon is colored, the shroud is monochrome; the brown color is more or less dark, because of the oxidation of the cellulose in the fabric.

These four religious factors then differ by reason of their forms and their specific finalities. Nevertheless, they have a point in common: they are all intelligible with reference to God, as signs and means of supernatural grace. These signs are not sacraments, for they have not been instituted by Jesus Christ, nor are they efficacious *ex opere operato* (that is, by reason of the work performed: the action engaging the infallible action of Christ Himself). They are signs of human making, intended to animate the faith and the works of the believer. They are efficacious *ex opere operantis* (dependent on the faith and the action of the believer who is their beneficiary, the grace of God helping along).

These signs are part of the divine pedagogy that leads mankind to God, to the invisible through what is visible, in accord with the sensible nature of man. They are part of the orbit of the Incarnation. God, Who made us in His image, was made visible to our eyes by becoming man. This foundational sign renewed, restructured and caused in large part the disappearance of the order of signs and forms of the Old Testament. Other Christian signs refer back to this sign-reality from which they derive all their value. They visibly link us to Heaven, the city of God, a universe that is invisible here below, one to which angels and saints belong.

Pilgrimages, shrines and icons are material, natural, objective signs; and apparitions are something apart, as signs that are formally supernatural, extraordinary, intimate, given to the seer, to the exclusion of those who are around the seer, and who do not see the apparition. This is why rational criticism tends to consider visions as subjective, as hallucinations or psychoanalytical projections:

"Whenever someone sees something which others do not see, I call that a hallucination, medically speaking," said Marc Oraison, a priest and doctor, not very open to the diversity of objective communications of which man is capable. Nevertheless, this objection raises problems of discernment.

We do not have to study these phenomena in themselves, but only in the measure that they concern the Blessed Virgin. This is a great measure, for in these four domains, Mary occupies a place of primary importance.

— 1. Shrines: for the Mother of the Lord is God's first dwelling among men, a living and holy dwelling, and therefore a shrine par excellence in the sense that we shall see later on. This is the reason why a record number of churches have been dedicated to her, from the very beginning of Christian shrines. Mary's importance is then well attested by Scripture and by a tradition of two thousand years.

— 2. Pilgrimages for the most part are directed towards places dedicated to the Blessed Virgin. Furthermore, she is the model of pilgrims under many titles, for, as we shall see, "each year" (*Luke* 2:41), in accord with the law, she made the pilgrimage to Jerusalem. Her entire destiny was an exemplary pilgrimage towards Heaven, the new Jerusalem (God's eternal sanctuary).

— 3. Icons often represent Mary. In this she surpasses all the other saints. This is understandable, for she made God visible to our eyes, in her image and her likeness.

She is therefore at the center of the mystery and also of Christian iconography. It is because of her mission to render God incarnate that the commandment of the Decalogue: "You shall not make a graven image" (*Ex.* 20:4) gives place to the need for icons and leads to the condemnation of iconoclasm, according to the principle enunciated by Theodore the Studite: "If art could not represent Christ, it would mean that the Word did not become incarnate" (3rd refutation pg. 99, 417C).

This is also why the Seventh Ecumenical Council (Nicaea II, 787), which reestablished the "holy images" against iconoclasm (Denzinger-Schönmetzer, 600-609), forbade the representation of the Father, invisible source of the divinity; and that is why iconography of the Holy Spirit remains difficult, ambiguous, an object of approximations, of errors and prohibitions, although the Gospel itself suggests the symbolism of the dove (*Matt.* 3:16; *Mark* 1:10; *John* 1:32).

— 4. As for apparitions, Mary is both their subject and object. At the Annunciation, she herself had if not an apparition, at least a locution (*Luke* 1:28-37), and had the benefit at least of Christ's final apparition at the Ascension (*Acts* 1:9-14). She is the object of the greater number of presumed apparitions, during modern times at any rate.

If, in certain theological and practical areas, the Blessed Virgin may appear to be on the margin or periphery, she is at the very center of the four topics of this book: by the double title of her close links with Christ and with us, as prototype of the Church, of faith in Jesus Christ, and of most charisms.

SIGNS OF POPULAR FAITH

These four subjects are connected as privileged signs of popular religion, for they are concrete, perceptible, human. The Christian people are not reached by abstraction alone. Not without reason, they prefer personal encounter and are attached to tangible signs that witness thereto. In this the *sensus fidelium* is seldom mistaken. It manifests its human dimension as well as its sense of the Incarnation.

SIGNS OF CONTRADICTION

These four types of signs have also been fought against and contested in various degrees. In different ways they are often signs of contradiction. This criticism is not a superficial and Modernist criticism. It is rooted in Revelation itself.

As regards the Temple, the theology and action of Jesus had scandalized the Jewish world, where the Temple was the sacred place par excellence, the very dwelling of the sacred. Jesus certainly showed His zeal for the "house of his Father" (*Luke* 1:48 and *John* 2:12-21), when He drove the buyers and sellers from the Temple, to purify it. But after that, He seems to invite its destruction. At any rate, that is how the judges interpreted Him during His trial (*Matt.* 26:61; *Mark* 14:58):

"I will destroy this temple made by hands."

But according to *John* 2:19, he spoke more precisely:

"Destroy this temple and in three days I will build it up."

He was speaking of the temple of His body, the Evangelist makes clear. He was predicting the time when the sanctuary of stone would disappear to make way for the living sanctuary, the physical and mystical body of Christ.

Jesus does away with the place of worship, therefore of the particular sanctuary, in the passage where he says to the Samaritan woman:

> *"The hour is coming when neither on this mountain nor in Jerusalem will you come to worship the Father, but [wherever] true adorers will adore the Father in Spirit and in truth"* (*John* 4:21).

Stephen, the first martyr, joins this revolutionary line of thought, at a time when Christians remained faithful to the Temple. To this holy place par excellence he applies the pejorative expression "made by human hands" (*Acts* 7:47-50).

This radical stance was not assumed by the Twelve at the beginning. The Apostles frequented the Temple with the purest traditional fervor (*Luke* 24:53; *Acts* 2:46; 3:1-10; 5:21-42), but they were rejected as a sect (*Acts* 24:5 and 14). From the beginning, their specifically Christian worship, the breaking of bread, was a domestic cult, foreign to the Temple.

The Jewish priests, rejected because of their conversion to Christianity, retained a nostalgia for the Temple. Paul's *Letter to the Hebrews* was written to have them overcome their regret, by showing them the fullness of the new worship in Jesus Christ, for He alone is priest and victim of the saving sacrifice, accomplished "outside" the Temple and completed in the heavenly sanctuary. In the year 70, the destruction of the Temple, predicted by Christ, thoroughly completed this removal, this rupture.

Pilgrimages as journeys to shrines was the object of those critics, who from the time of the Devotio Moderna (the fourteenth century) to the Reformation, raged: "What good is it to seek God here or there, since the place of His presence is none other than the conscious life of man, whether personal or communitarian."

> "*Where two or three are gathered together in my name, there am I in the midst of them*" (*Matt.* 18:20).

The criticism of images is more ancient and more radical. The second commandment of the Decalogue forbids them (*Deut.* 27:15; *Exod.* 20:4; *Deut.* 4:9-28). The Bible condemns images made by the hands of men and opposes them to the works of God the Creator. It is not statues "made by human hands" (*Deut.* 4:8), but creation, the work of God, that makes God known (*Hosea* 8:58; *Wis.*

13; *Rom.* 1:19-23). It is not through the intermediary of images that God allows Himself to be moved, but heart to heart.

Iconoclasm is founded on this precept, supported by Jewish and Islamic influence. It was fostered by Manichaeism which stated: If matter is evil, it cannot join us to the divine. And there were heresies about the Incarnation: Nestorianism (which separates the two natures in Christ), is inclined towards naturalistic representations; Monophysitism (which absorbs the humanity into the divinity), is inclined on the contrary to transfigure human representation.

These two tendencies, which traverse Christian iconography, are acceptable if they are held within certain limits. For example, the first one insists on the humility of Christ in line with Isaiah. So the Christ of Rouault, resembling the sad clowns, relates to: *"Object of contempt, abandoned by men, a man of sorrows, acquainted with suffering"* (*Is.* 53:2-3). The second tendency exalts His majesty as at Tahull (1123), or at the cathedral of Autun, and even in the blazing representations of El Greco.

Between the two deformations, Christian iconography presents a transfiguration in realism.

Apparitions are devalued by this maxim of Christ: *"Blessed are those who have not seen and have believed"* (*John* 20:29).

This devaluation of visions is stressed in the Church for fear that the seers will set themselves up as a parallel magisterium, or else sink into the real risks of illumnism.

From Lourdes to Medjugorje, these unusual phenomena are ordinarily perceived by the establishment as bad news, and as an abnormal intrusion. These prejudices harden at a time when apparitions abound, stimulated by a revival of spiritual hunger, at a time when spirituality and discernment are in a state of crisis within the Church.

THE POINT OF VIEW OF COMPARATIVE RELIGION

Pilgrimages and shrines, images and apparitions are religious phenomena that are widely spread, even apart from Christianity. It would be interesting to study the phenomenon inductively, from the point of view of comparative religion and sociology. We will limit ourselves to the essential, to the Christian aspect, in order to grasp its meaning, for such is the first mission of theology. In this chapter the important thing is what Revelation has disentangled from magic, doctrine from mythology, worship from ritual formalism.

In what order should we treat these four interconnected subjects? From the point of view of Christian revelation, to which we will limit ourselves, it would seem logical to begin with shrines, towards which pilgrimages make their way.

Still, the history of the people of God, wandering on pilgrimage, moves from a nomad existence to a stationary location (the creation or the anarchic adaptation of shrines in Canaan was resolved by the establishment of the one and only Temple in Jerusalem). From this there will result a religion of pilgrimages to Jerusalem, that will end with the destruction of the Temple and a new theology of the shrine within Christianity. We will begin therefore with pilgrimages in accord with what came first. Images, which appear only within Christianity, slowly and not without some reaction, will be treated third, in keeping with the same principle. And apparitions, last of all, for they are a phenomenon apart. If they belong to the theology of the image as icons do, they are not at all among the images that can be grasped objectively. These images come from God and from the one who experiences them in an interiority that is inaccessible.

PART II

CHAPTER 1

Pilgrimages

DEFINITION AND STRUCTURE

The word "pilgrimage" comes from the Latin *peregrinus*. *Peregrinus* means "stranger," for the pilgrim is a traveler. He has left his home in order to come to a country (or a place) that is not his own. It is then from these shrines that he has received this name.

Etymologically, the word has its root *per ager:* one who goes through a field, or one who goes across a frontier. In doing so, the traveler becomes a stranger, going to a place not his own.

Biblical theology highlights this etymology. The First Letter of Peter invites us to consider ourselves here below as people without a country, on pilgrimage to Heaven, our one true home.

> *"I exhort you as strangers and pilgrims to abstain from carnal desires that war against the soul"* (*1 Peter* 2:11).

Similarly the Epistle to the Hebrews 11:13-16:

> *In the way of faith all these [the Hebrews] died without receiving the promises [the promised land], but beholding them from afar*

9

*off and saluting them and acknowledging that
they were pilgrims and strangers on earth...
seeking a homeland. If they were thinking of the
country from which they went out, they would
have had opportunity to return there. But as it
is, they seek a better, that is a heavenly country.*

An earthly pilgrimage is a rehearsal for the great pilgrimage of life. It places us as a traveler on the road to
Heaven. The Apostle Paul uses the same concept of
stranger, but in order to underline that Christ has already
rescued us from this condition, and to make us citizens
with the saints even here below (*Eph.* 2:19; *Col.* 1:21).

The word "pilgrim" has come to mean more specifically one who travels in order to visit a holy place. But
at the present time, its meaning has been expanded to
include significant places that mere memory has hallowed:
— the country of one's youth or of one's ancestors. So
    many Americans go on pilgrimage to their Irish or
    German roots, and certain Hispanics go to Spain, to
    Portugal, or to one of the countries of Latin America.
— an inspiring or impressive site, one of the world's
    marvels.
— the place where an important event took place: the
    allied invasion of Normandy in 1944 or the birthplace
    or the tomb of a great man.

Stalin, at great expense, had the corpse of Lenin
embalmed to expose it in a mausoleum in Red Square,
before which the crowds passed in an endless line with
more solemnity than at Rome before the tomb of the
Apostles.

To some extent there have been pilgrimages throughout
time and space. For example, among the ancient Greeks
there was the cult of Apollo, god of medicine. Among
the Jews, there were the biblical sites associated with the
patriarchs or the prophets: Hebron (place of the alliance
with Abraham), Haran (the place of Jacob's dream of
promise, which he renamed Beth-el, House of God), and

the western wall of the Temple and the Talmudic tombs.

For Muslims, of prime importance is Mecca, birthplace of the prophet (570-632). In 1982, several million Muslims had made their pilgrimage *(haji)* to the ka'ba (the well and dwelling of Abraham, venerated before the advent of Islam). But Islam also has other places of pilgrimage: first of all, Medina, tomb of the prophet, and Jerusalem, where the mosque El Ashra is the place of the prophet's ascension (ib. 338-346).

Buddhists feel an interior pilgrimage has more value than an exterior one. The main one is Bodh Gaya, where Buddha received enlightenment. But there are many Buddhist pilgrimages throughout South Asia and the East. It is the same with most other religions (and nationalities) as well.

Pilgrimage implies three elements that are closely connected.

1. THE POINT OF DEPARTURE: This is where the pilgrim lives. We leave our ordinary life and break with our environment, our roots, our habits, our home, in order to take on the condition of a stranger.

2. THE ROAD from the point of departure to the point of arrival. To go on foot is the natural way, but other means of transport are possible: horse, bicycle, boat, car, train, plane, etc., in short, any vehicle imaginable. The journey is an image of human life.

3. THE END: that is, the place of arrival. Its sacred character sets off a pilgrimage specifically from other kinds of journeys. To this, one may add what happens after a pilgrimage, which can be a spiritual conversion or else a return to the condition which one left.

The structure of all this is quite simple. The analysis of any story is the identification of joining and separation that mark its development. The fable of the fox and the crow begins with the joining of the crow and the cheese, then the separation to the benefit of the fox, the flatterer who makes it his own: a new joining. A pilgrimage is a separation from a profane place, where sin abounds, to form a symbolic joining with a sacred place.

This process is called "conversion." The word accurately identifies the Greek, *metanoia,* often found in the Gospel, which signifies a turning around. This word conversion has been taken in its etymological sense in the language used in skiing, where it means a 180 degree turn during a descent by pivoting the lower ski. We turn away from evil, from self-regarding egoism to turn ourself toward God. We break with the profane for a conjunction with God, which is what the holy place chosen as the goal of the journey symbolizes. Thus **conversion** and **penance** are the key words that are found in the very short message of Lourdes: "penance (repent) for the conversion of sinners" (24 February 1858). This is the essential element of a pilgrimage. This interior revolution, inspired by God, Who is the master of the dance, is a pure gift of grace, as opposed to something achieved by the pilgrim. The final conjunction is both rest in God and a source of new powers for a new kind of life. The pilgrimage then, has as its aim to recreate or to strengthen our bonds with God.

Christian pilgrimages then are prolonged rites, intended to vivify the course of human life toward God. They outline the program of human destiny, which moves from an earthly birth, to a birth in Heaven, for we are created by God to return to God.

The pilgrimage of human life is less a change of "place" than of "condition." It is the course for a spiritual combat (against mediocrity, lukewarmness, and the forces of evil), during which transcendant love ought to penetrate, transform, and transfigure life in all its dimensions, each moment of our existence and every area of our being even our subconscious. Life is a dramatic journey.

At the end of the journey, death is a new birth. It reveals communion with God. This identification is brought about in the night of faith, just as the caterpillar becomes a butterfly in the folds and darkness of its chrysalis. After our earthly life, God, Who is spirit, becomes visible immediately, face to face as St. Paul says (*1 Cor.* 13:1-2), not only as Creator at the root of our being, but as a friend, who lifts us up to Himself, by communicating to us, in all fullness and interiority, His life of knowledge and love. Pilgrimages, which highlight and punctuate the existence of Christians are like a rehearsal for this great journey which ends in the meeting with God.

A pilgrimage miniaturizes and embodies these same three stages of life:

1. THE DEPARTURE brings about the initial break, for free time to be given entirely to God.

2. THE JOURNEY inspired by faith is an ascetical and mystical road toward God, marked by spiritual growth as one draws near the destination.

3. ARRIVAL at the holy place, where one meets God through the eloquent symbols of the shrine, where one dwells with him.

The sacred place (the location or shrine), with its images, is the recollection of the house of God, where His presence becomes perceptible. Often, there is venerated in that place a spring, more or less miraculous, an eloquent sign that may refresh, heal, or purify. It is also a memorial.

The location is often very beautiful: "The Blessed Virgin has good taste," said Louis Veuillot on arriving at the mountainous and undulating country around Lourdes. The same can be said of Medjugorje, or La Salette.

The ceremonies actualize the faith and processions of all kinds abound—Masses, Rosaries, the Way of the Cross, Reconciliation.

A pilgrimage is an absorbing experience. It is spontaneously a time of openness, of generosity, of conversion, and often of beautiful new friendships.

The pastoral problem that remains is what happens after the pilgrimage—the return home, that it not be a reversal, a falling once again into mediocrity or sin, but a continual conversion for a new life, one of prayer, and of one taken up with the service of the Lord. It is the good of all pilgrimages, and has been since Old Testament times.

CHAPTER 2

Historic Beginnings of Pilgrimages

The pilgrimage, symbol in miniature of the great journey of human life toward God, has an important place in the Bible, under forms that are infinitely diversified through such fundamental human things as places, symbols, signs, calls and motivations. The frontier shifts between the journey between nomadic life and pilgrimage properly so called.

The people of God begin by wanderings. Abraham, a semi-nomad shepherd, moved from pasture to pasture on a planet a thousand times less populated than it is today, where there were vast open spaces. The call that God directed to him was an invitation to a journey. He removed him from his pagan land to another place, where God formed him, both him and his descendants.

"Leave your country, your family and your father's house for the land that I will show you. I will make of you a great nation" (*Gen.* 12:1-2).

God speaks of a **place**, but going further, of a **future.** The pilgrimage brings together space and time. His pilgrimage is marked by encounters with God (*Gen.* 12:7) on land of which his posterity will take possession only six centuries later. His itinerary is guided from the interior by a complete hope and by an unconditional faith, which a slow and gradual revelation will instruct, a revelation intended for him and for his people. The places of his testing and above all the places of the covenant will, for future generations, become places of pilgrimage.

But, during the age of the patriarchs, the only pilgrimage properly so called was the one that God demanded that Jacob make to Bethel (*Gen.* 35:1-10), where God revealed Himself to him when he was fleeing from his brother (*Gen.* 28:10-15). At that time he expelled the strange gods from his household, and God confirmed the new name which He had given him after his heavenly combat: "Israel" (that is, strong as with God) (*Gen.* 35:10).

EXODUS

The fixed abode in Egypt, where the sons of Israel multiplied and grew into a nation, became a place of slavery. The liberation inaugurated an arduous pilgrimage lasting about a half century (roughly from 1250 to 1200 B.C.). The people had no sanctuary in Egypt, nor after they crossed the Red Sea and arrived at Sinai. According to the Bible, itinerancy is the initial condition of the chosen people. The Exodus was a long march with God: forty years, strewn with trials, toward the place predestined, a new earthly paradise flowing with milk and honey (*Deut.* 8:7 ff.).

After the revelation on Sinai, the Lord came to live in the midst of his people in the tent that sheltered the Ark of the Covenant. He shared Israel's itinerant state, beneath a tent in their midst.

The Exodus does not formally fulfill the idea of a pilgrimage, which is a journey to a holy place. The Promised Land is not yet holy, but pagan. It will have to be conquered, sanctified, and purified by the people, who are already a place made holy by the presence of God in their midst. The Exodus then was a pilgrimage by analogy, paradoxically. The meaning of the sacred is somehow reversed. It is the pilgrims who are its guardians and are going to conquer a world that is desacralized. In 587 B.C.

a new captivity called for a new liberation and a new exodus.

Second, Isaiah presents it as such, marked by similar miracles. God calls the unhappy people to renew their courage and to prepare to leave. As the Red Sea did formerly, so now the Euphrates will divide so that the liberated people pass through. The Lord will be the guide and a way will be made in the desert. God will make water spring up as formerly at Meriba and the desert will be changed into an orchard. This time, it will really be a pilgrimage, toward a holy place, desecrated and destroyed during the conquest, and that is going to be rebuilt (*Isaiah,* Chapters 35 to 41).

John the Baptist will take up these themes in order to urge the people to prepare for the coming of the Messiah, as though in a liberating march through the desert (*Luke* 3:4-6). But what is meant is a moral preparation of hearts for the one who is coming.

In the Bible, the notion of journey (pilgrimages) takes many forms and provides many companions.

PILGRIMAGES IN THE PROMISED LAND

If the Bible singles out only one pilgrimage, properly speaking, before the settlement in the Promised Land (*Gen.* 35:1-10, cited above), and if the Exodus was a pilgrimage only by analogy, the idea is borne out in its proper sense after the settlement in the Promised Land.

Then pilgrimages appeared to numerous shrines: Gilgal, Sichem, Macpelah, Silo, etc. Historians and archaeologists tend to think that these were pagan shrines, converted more or less completely to Yahwism by the glorious emplacement of the Ark of the Covenant.

Exegetes wonder in what measure the adoption of the pagan shrines, especially those of the Canaanites, was made legitimate by the holy actions of the fathers. There were venerated:

— their altars (*Gen.* 12:7 ff.; 13:4; 26:25; 33:20)

— their pillars (*Gen.* 28:18)
— their sacred trees (*Gen.* 12:6; 18:1; 21:33)
— There the pilgrim would perform these rites:
    invoke the name of Yahweh under various titles
      (*Gen.* 12:8; 13:4; 21:33; 33:20)
    anoint with oil (*Gen.* 28:18; 35:14)
    perform purifications (*Gen.* 35:2 ff.)
    pay tithes (*Gen.* 14:20 and 28:22).

In the following sections, we see how all these shrines were progressively fought against, eclipsed, and replaced by the setting up of the one sanctuary in the capital, Jerusalem, where Solomon built the temple for the Ark of the Covenant, which ended by supplanting the other shrines.

All the Israelites were required to come there three times a year. But custom reduced these three pilgrimages to only one for the distant regions such as Galilee (*Luke* 2:41). By way of compensation, women and children took part, as did Mary and Jesus (from *Luke* 2:40 to *John* 19:25-27), from pilgrimages in His infancy, to that of His death.

NEW TESTAMENT

Pilgrimages hold an important place in the life of Jesus.

According to the prescriptions cited from Exodus, each year, from His infancy, He made the pilgrimage to Jerusalem for the feast of the Passover. It was during the Passover pilgrimage when He was twelve years old that He gave the first prophetic sign of His Passion (*Luke* 2:40-50).

Throughout His life, He practiced the Jewish religion: from the circumcision to the ceremony of the Presentation, and to the Passover celebrated on the eve of His death. He practiced as a layman and not as a priest.

The Gospel of John is built around the narration of pilgrimages Jesus made to Jerusalem during His public life:
— Passover (*John* 2:13-24)
— perhaps Pentecost with the cure of the man at the pool of Bethsaida (*John* 5)

— second Passover (*John* 6:4)

— the Jewish Feast of Booths (*John* 7): with the promise of the living water and the cure of the blind man

— Feast of the Dedication (*John* 10:22)

— finally the third Passover: that of the Passion (*John* 11:55; 19:42)

The Jews, the baptized proselytes, especially the priests who became Christians, were separated from the Temple and cut off from a pilgrimage forbidden to them. The Letter to the Hebrews (written around the year 60) responds to their nostalgia by teaching them that the sacrifices of Jesus, completed in Heaven, renders void the Temple of Jerusalem. Its destruction was foretold by Christ.

BEYOND PILGRIMAGES

This destruction ended the pilgrimages to Jerusalem. For Christians, the cultic umbilical cord was, as it were, cut. At first they had frequented the Temple through tradition. But their specific form of worship, instituted by Jesus Christ on the eve of His death with the breaking of bread, had no need of a temple.

THE BEGINNING OF CHRISTIAN PILGRIMAGES

Very quickly pilgrimages were reborn in the Church, for they are inscribed within man's condition as one who is on a journey in history, in memories and in biblical symbolism. Origen (ca. 185-254) informs us that the grotto and the crib at Bethlehem were venerated in his days.

The tombs of the martyrs and then those of the confessors became holy places, goals of pilgrimages. At Nazareth, another place associated with the infancy, a graffito of the third century, recalls the angel's greeting to Mary, *Chaire Maria* (Rejoice, Mary; cf. *Luke* 1:28).

It was after the conversion of Constantine to Christianity (314), which then became the state religion, that pilgrimages began to develop, first of all back to Jerusalem, the place of origin.

After returning from the Council of Nicaea (325), the

bishop of Jerusalem undertook excavations to find the Holy Sepulcher in a city ravaged by the Romans after the second revolt of 132-135. Helen, mother of the Emperor, made the pilgrimage herself, built basilicas at Bethlehem and the Mount of Olives (Eusebius, *The Life of Constantine* 3:30, p. 20, 1080) and discovered the true cross. The Emperor immediately ordered the construction of a basilica on the site of the discovery at the expense of the public treasury. Other churches were built at Bethlehem, Tabor, Hebron, Capharnaum, and elsewhere, which became places of pilgrimage. The tombs of the martyrs and of the confessors established other places of pilgrimage, as did the tombs of the Blessed Virgin at Gethsemane, that of John the Baptist at Sebaste, of John the Evangelist at Ephesus, of Euphemia at Chalcedon, etc.

At Rome, people visited the tombs of Peter and Paul, over which two basilicas are built in their honor. St. Peter's, at the Vatican, was built as early as 337. The catacombs were cared for. The veneration of the saints took form.

The number of pilgrims was numerous, and people spoke of their pilgrimages, beginning with Helen, mother of the Emperor. These travelers belonged to all social strata, from kings to ordinary people, and included women. Some have left accounts of their journeys.

Author Pierre Maraval enumerates their motives: "to pray, to see, to be instructed, to bolster their knowledge of Scripture and their defense of the faith, to be edified at the tombs of the martyrs or near the monks, to adore, to receive power from relics, to obtain various kinds of favors, notably cures, to give thanks, to do penance or even to settle permanently in these places" (p. 137-151, *Lieux saints et pelerinages d' Orient*, 1985).

Some pilgrims went as far as Egypt to visit the hermits in the desert, or the famous stylites such as Simon at Qualat in northern Syria.

In 638, when Jerusalem was conquered by the Muslims,

pilgrimages become rare, but they flourished at Constantinople, where the true cross had been transported. The cult of relics also begins.

THE MIDDLE AGES

The Middle Ages, avid for relics, multiplied them, took them from place to place, and sometimes stole them. This also established places of pilgrimage. Charlemagne and his successors protected pilgrims and the pilgrimage to Rome became important.

Countless were the pilgrimages to the shrine of Archangel Saint Michael. This cult was founded on some Jewish traditions before our era. He is the archangel who conducts souls before the throne of God, according to the second *Book of Enoch,* 22:4-6 and the *Gospel of Nicodemus.* In the Judeo-Christian, *History of Joseph the Carpenter,* the adoptive father of Jesus asks for the help of the Archangel for his pilgrimage across the sea.

This cult is widespread, for the monogram XMG (Christ, Michael, Gabriel) is attested to from the beginning of the fourth century among the Syrians, the Egyptians and even in the Italian peninsula.

One of the most ancient is the pilgrimage to Mount Gargan, which assumed a great importance beginning on May 8, 663, when the Lombards crushed the Saracen fleet after invoking St. Michael. This pilgrimage, with an international appeal, became restricted to Italy with the founding of Mont Saint Michel in Normandy, where Richard I established a Benedictine monastery in 966.

In the ninth century, the "discovery" of the body of the Apostle St. James at Compostella, instituted the most important pilgrimage of the Middle Ages, which continued and extended despite the destruction of the basilica by the arms of the redoubtable Al Mancour in 997. The site was reconquered from the Moors and the rebuilt sanctuary became a beacon for all Christendom with a series of jubilees, the first of which took place at the beginning of the twelfth century and the apogee in the thirteenth.

The pilgrim roads converged from all over Europe and their lengths, strewn with remarkable monuments, have not been forgotten. The young, called together by John Paul II, made them their own in 1987.

Then there was a series of the crusades: military pilgrimages to reconquer and guard the tomb of Christ.

In England the assassination of St. Thomas Becket, on December 22, 1170, also brought about a flood of pilgrims to the cathedral, the place of his martyrdom.

In the eleventh century there began the development of pilgrimages honoring the Blessed Virgin, to whom the chief Gothic cathedrals were dedicated: Chartres, Le Puy, Paris, Clermont, Boulogne, Montserrat and many other local shrines, Notre Dame de Liesse, Our Lady of Walsingham in England, Our Lady of Mariazell in Austria. Notre Dame de Rocamadour saw a great expansion after the discovery of the presumed body of the hermit Saint Amadour in 1166.

This multiplication of pilgrimages in France put the pilgrimage to Rome, and also the one to Compostella, in the background.

MODERN CRITICISM AND THE DECLINE DURING THE RENAISSANCE

The multiplication of pilgrimages continued into the fourteenth century and beyond. But the age of criticism had begun. At the end of the fourteenth century, John Wyclif, Gerard Groote and Jean Gerson, created the *Modern Devotions,* which interiorized faith and devalued these popular expressions, these travelers ostensibly on pilgrimage.

In the sixteenth century, the Christian humanists Erasmus and Rabelais, pressed increasingly sarcastic attacks against these offensive and useless journeys.

The Protestant Reform, which preached faith alone, grace alone, Scripture alone, Christ alone, God alone, fought inherently against pilgrimages in both word and act. In 1562, the Huguenots at Tours burned the body of St. Martin, apostle of the Gauls.

THE RENAISSANCE, THE COUNTER REFORMATION, THE END OF THE SIXTEENTH CENTURY

The leaders of the Catholic Counter Reformation were in accord with reformers in stigmatizing abuses. In 1604 St. Robert Bellarmine and Father Richehôme (1544-1628) condemned those who "while on pilgrimage lead a dis-ordered life" or who "scour the land without devotion" (in short, tourists before that term was invented). But they also gave new value to the true reasons for pilgrimages: to honor God, to do penance, "to endure the incon-veniences of the road; to imitate the fine examples of the saints whom one is visiting" (G. Reiter, *Heiligenverehrung und Wallfahrt,* Wurzburg, 1970, p. 202).

The climate was favorable for a renewal of pilgrimages, beginning with that to Rome, which Pope Paul III (1534-1549) promoted. The high point was the pilgrimage to the Holy House of Loreto, which, be it noted, Mon-taigne visited in 1581, Descartes between 1623 and 1625, and then Grignion de Montfort in May-June 1706.

It also saw the rapid development of Our Lady of Guadalupe at the place of the apparitions in Mexico in 1531.

In Europe, there was Saint Anne d'Auray and Notre Dame de Grâce at Rochefort-du-Gard. In the south of France is was Notre Dame de Lumières at the foot of Lubéron.

SEVENTEENTH AND EIGHTEENTH CENTURIES

Monarchy did not care for this multiplicity of vaga-bonds along the roads. King Louis XIV published several edicts:

> against the disorders that are introduced into the kingdom under a specious pretext of devotion and of pilgrimages [. . .]. The abuse is such that

some so-called pilgrims leave their parents and their family against their wishes, leave their wife and children without any help, steal from their master, abandon their apprenticeship and, following the spirit of licentiousness that inspired them, pass the course of their pilgrimage in continual debauchery. It even happens that the greater number of vagabonds and vagrants, assume the character of pilgrims in order to continue in their laziness move along in this company, from province to province, and make a public profession of mendicancy (Ordonnance of 27 August 1671).

These edicts respected the principle of pilgrimages, but intended "to repress only the corruption of a thing that is so holy."

They therefore subjected this practice to formal authorizations and passports, violations being given appropriate punishments ranging from the iron collar to flogging, to the galleys, depending on the seriousness of the infraction and repetition of the offense.

Repression must not have been very effective since it was necessary to multiply the edicts and their reprinting throughout the seventeenth and eighteenth centuries. Local functionaries sometimes were quite active. The assistant to the administrator at Pau disparaged pilgrimages as "pretexts for an infinite number of vagabonds, who go to St. James of Compostella in order to commit many excesses there."

Despite everything, this popular phenomenon remained alive. The books of various confraternities attest to that, despite the fact that during this time the pilgrim hostels were closed or transformed into hospitals. Modern economic development is incompatible with the wandering of exiles on the road to Heaven. Only earthly realities and domestic virtues are cultivated. Spiritual evolution is measured by material progress—today's standards.

The stance against pilgrimages converged with the more radical one of the philosophies of the eighteenth century. Diderot's *Encyclopédie* defined pilgrimages as a journey "of mistaken devotion." In Germany, the Enlightenment influenced kings in the same way. Joseph II in Austria and Karl Theodore in Bavaria forbade or severely controlled processions and pilgrimages which "encouraged laziness, disorder and vagabondage." "Let us stamp out the vile beast," said Voltaire (*Correspondance* 28 November 1762, p. 112).

The French Revolution radicalized the opposition to pilgrimages. It closed or destroyed shrines, dissolved confraternities, secularized religious, and persecuted in all kinds of ways. The wars of the Empire promoted the pillaging of various places of pilgrimage. The retrogression reached its lowest point at the beginning of the nineteenth century.

FROM THE RENAISSANCE TO THE NINETEENTH CENTURY

It was in 1830 that the re-awakening and the alteration of pilgrimages began. During his lifetime, the radiance of St. John Mary Vianney made his small parish a place for an original kind of pilgrimage, founded not on the holiness of a place or on a past event, but on meeting with a living saint, with a charismatic confessor. People went to confession there and were converted by the charism of the Curé of Ars.

Following the apparition of the Blessed Virgin in the chapel of the rue du Bac, in Paris, on 27 November 1830, the Miraculous Medal was struck at the end of May, 1832. It surpassed the record for all medals: a million copies by the time St. Catherine Labouré died in 1876, and today many millions in all.

Then came La Salette in 1846; Lourdes in 1858; Pontmain in 1871, etc. Finally, other ancient shrines were reborn and prospered: Rocamadour, Bétharam, Garaison.

Modern transportation by train, steamship and the

development of tourism stimulated pilgrimages. They entered the channels of a consolidated industry whose growth equals that of the largest enterprises. The risks and discomfort diminished. The number of travelers increased in astronomical proportions. The dreams and desires for travel were cultivated in all directions and included such non-religious motivations as the exploration of other worlds (cf. *Around the World in Eighty Days,* by Jules Verne), political or cultural objectives, visits to archeological sites, curiosity, a taste for the exotic, etc. Our century has even come to sex tours promoted by some Asiatic countries. The Church would have been mistaken to abandon trips to just secular enterprises. On the contrary, she was way ahead in the development of travel. She exploited new possibilities to arrange trips for religious ends.

The great development took place in the second half of the nineteenth century. The pioneers were the Assumptionists: Father Emmanuel d'Alzon and his young assistant, François Picard, who would become the second superior general. On January 24, 1872, he laid the foundation for the Association Notre Dame du Salut, to assure the salvation of France with special attention to the world of the working class. France became a pilot country for pilgrimages whose forms she developed and multiplied in a Christian sense that was exacting and free of glamorous attraction. They looked to history and to the presence of Christ and of his Mother.

This Association nationalized pilgrimages and started them again, at an unprecedented rate. On August 22, 1872, a gathering of 375 priests at La Salette founded the Counseil général des pèlerinages (General Council for Pilgrimages) directed by Father Picard. That same year, Lourdes received 119,000 pilgrims brought in by 178 special trains—a considerable feat for the French railroads. There is no account of the number of pilgrimages for that year.

The year 1873 augmented this movement even further.

In that year 216 special trains brought to Lourdes 140,000 pilgrims from forty-seven dioceses. At the same time, the annual *Pèlerinage national de Lourdes* (The Lourdes National Pilgrimage) was founded, held 21-25 July, and which continues to this day. The famous White Train was inaugurated (a hospital on rails). This was a new dimension for pilgrimages, for it transported the sick to Lourdes by rail.

In 1882, Father Picard led 1,013 pilgrims in two steamships: *La Picardie* and *La Guadeloupe,* on a special pilgrimage by sea. It was an austere trip. Father Picard exacted from all the participants a promise of obedience, like a religious vow. The two ships were two floating convents where an immense cross was set up. There was prayer, sermons, ways of the cross, liturgical services, all fifteen decades of the rosary—these succeeded each other during the week on the sea until docking at Jaifa. From there a pilgrimage was made to seventeen places, on foot and not on horseback (J. Chelini, *Les chemins de Dieu,* p. 341). The Assumptionists eventually built a magnificent hospice for pilgrims in Jerusalem.

They established a notable press corps to encourage pilgrimages and a weekly publication, *La Croix,* which still exists but is very much secularized. Apart from piety, these pilgrimages to the Holy Land intended to confront the "invasion of the holy places" by the Greeks and the schismatic Russians, who overwhelmed the Catholic Church, which was little represented. It amounted to a "new and peaceful crusade to reconquer Jerusalem, rosary in hand." The country was grateful for this manna.

But the anti-religious laws of France in 1880 and in 1901-1904 confiscated the goods of the Church, expelled the teaching religious, and so struck a blow at shrines and pilgrimages. Anti-clericalism was rampant also in Germany, Spain and Portugal. The movement, that was thus shackled, still remained alive.

The death of Thérèse of the Infant Jesus, at the age

of twenty-four, in 1897, gave rise at the beginning of the twentieth century to a new pilgrimage to Lisieux. Modern forms of pilgrimage did not die out, but gave rise to heroic forms on foot. Before the war of 1914, at a time when the automobile began to master the roads, they began long marches from Paris to the cathedral of Chartres, a distance of eighty kilometers.

The apparitions in Fatima, Portugal, in 1917, produced pilgrims by the tens of thousands, then by millions. The great development of the area skyrocketed after the war of 1940-1945. This period also saw apparitions officially approved in Beauraing and Banneux in Belgium, during 1932-1933.

During and immediately after the second world war, a new kind of pilgrimage evolved. It was no longer the faithful who traveled, but the statue of Our Lady. It spread through France and set in motion gigantic missions of prayer and penance. In the United States, the movement became more profound. Under the direction of John Haffert, the Blue Army was inaugurated. Its members quickly totalled in the millions as the movement spread worldwide. The statue of Our Lady of Fatima (the Pilgrim Virgin) soon started visiting every country following massive tours across the United States. The concept of pilgrimage was reaching the apex of its development.

At Vatican Council II, certain of the intelligentsia predicted the death of pilgrimage, particularly the fanatic spirituality of Fatima and Lourdes. But to the complete contrary, the development expanded. After Vatican II, the number of pilgrims going to Lourdes rose from two to six million annually; while the number of sick who come has increased and diversified, extending gradually to all kinds of categories, including the mentally handicapped and those confined to hospitals because of the constraints of dialysis or artificial respiration. In the debacle that followed the Council, Lourdes became a spiritual harbor, a refuge of earnest and disinterested prayer. Fatima, in

Portugal, matched it. Pilgrimage was "in."

Taizé, a Protestant and ecumenical monastery, founded in 1945, has drawn crowds of young people, who have been so neglected in the post-conciliar Church.

Beginning in 1981, the multiplication of apparitions gave rise to new pilgrimages: in the first place at Medjugorje, which, despite the opposition of Bishop Zanic, battling with the Franciscans and the Communist government, had attained a magnitude slightly superior to those of Fatima: more than a million communions a year, with a world record of confessions and conversions.

TYPOLOGY OF PILGRIMAGES

Fundamental studies have not presented a developed typology (symbolism) about Catholic pilgrimages.

For a preliminary study, two principal groups stand out:

1. Tombs, from early times. In the Holy Land, those of the patriarchs and of Christ; in Rome, those of Peter and Paul and of so many martyrs. A number of pilgrimages connected with apparitions fall into this category: Rue du Bac, where the shrine of St. Catherine Labouré is venerated; at Nevers, that of St. Bernadette of Lourdes; at Lisieux, that of Thérèse of the Child Jesus.

Some American pilgrimages also belong to this group: St. Rose and St. Martin de Porres in Lima, Peru, St. John Neumann in Philadelphia, Blessed Philippine Duchesne at St. Charles, Missouri, and Mother Cabrini in New York City.

Also included here, though more rarely, are pilgrimages to places where the seers lived: Catherine Labouré at Faint-les-Moutiers, and Thérèse of Lisieux at Alençon during their childhood; Mother Cabrini at Denver, and others.

2. Pilgrimages have been made to persons still living, reputed for their holiness, their charisms, their oracles or their apparitions. So in times past, people visited the fathers of the desert; during the nineteenth century, the Curé of Ars; in our own day, Father Jozo Zovko, O.F.M.,

pastor at Medjugorje at the beginning of the apparitions, who has caused as many pilgrimages to the place to which he has been transferred as to Medjugorje. But the personalities of preachers, great charismatics, or healers, equally draw crowds.

Apparitions, whether recognized or not, lay the foundations for the most important pilgrimages in the world, especially apparitions of the Blessed Virgin to which we shall return. Apparitions of the Sacred Heart of Jesus to Margaret Mary Alacoque in the seventeenth century is a principal exception.

Other shrines commemorate events:
— victories or protection from harm.
— cures: sometimes for a particular malady, sometimes for all kinds of cures, as at Lourdes.
— miracles: notably eucharistic miracles, which are often dreaded today.
— pictures or statues.
— the shedding of perfumed oil (icons of Mary, Gate of Heaven, at Montreal and at Toulouse, of Soufanieh at Damascus) or of tears, blood, or sweat (all three at Akita, Japan).

This symbolism is difficult to elaborate, for these different factors often either interfere with each other, or succeed, or come together in the same pilgrimage. At Lourdes we venerate the memory of the apparitions of 1858. But we venerate also the mill where Bernadette was born, the cachot, the town jail of her wretched childhood at the time of the apparitions, and the last home of her parents. People also come to ask for cures, which have a very great importance at Lourdes.

At Akita, Japan, there are sheddings (of tears, etc.) but also messages, and the seer, a victim soul, is also sought after.

The last three decades of this century have spawned an enormous growth in this concept of pilgrimage. Certainly, the increased crescendo of claimed apparitions is the major factor. Not all of these apparition sites proved worthy of the cult developed and caused much confusion in the Church and in the laity (Bayside, New York, for example). Others have produced undeniable fruits through a following unprecedented in size.

Medjugorje, in the former country of Yugoslavia, is the most notable example. This tiny hamlet, tucked away in the low mountains of a rural countryside, saw supernatural manifestations beginning in June of 1981, mushroom into worldwide prominence. Within 10 years, 15,000,000 people had come from all over the world. It became known as the reconciliation (Sacrament of Confession) center of the world.

By the arrival of the last decade of this century, apparitions were being claimed all over the world. America suddenly emerged as the forerunner, providing relatively easy access to people for pilgrimage right in their own country.

CHAPTER 3

Objections to Pilgrimages

We have seen how pilgrimages developed. Here is a typology of common objections to pilgrimages and their meaning (significance).

STERILITY (USELESSNESS)

Pilgrimages are claimed to be uselessness. "What is the use of that time lost, this abandonment of professional and family responsibilities?"

If these reasons have some merit and deserve attention, what is freely given by God does have its price. In the Gospel, the protest: *"To what purpose is this waste?"* comes from Judas (*John* 12:5; cf. *Matt.* 26:8). "Losses" are part of all human life, where diversions and vacations have their normal place, and exploits of all kinds seem to meet with approval, such as the crossing of the Pacific by Gerard d'Aboville in 1992.

"What was the good of it?" some objected after his first performance (crossing the Atlantic in 1980).

"For nothing, for myself,' he answered.

Mystics answer "for God, for mankind, for the salvation of the world." Gratuitousness is essential in our relations with God.

The accusation of uselessness has also been leveled against monks and hermits. This disparages their generally laborious lives and the services they undertake or inspire in so many ways. If other forms of leisure get good press, why are pilgrimages considered blameworthy? Why should not a trip to please God have some appeal?

MATERIALISTIC PIETY

The materializing of popular piety has often been criticized. What good is it to set store by a place, to touch or kiss the rock of the Grotto at Lourdes? The meaning (of a place) has been profoundly changed. Christian prayer and liturgy redirect hope in a transcendant God, beyond any kind of supposed material powers. Lacade, the mayor at Lourdes in 1858, had obtained a favorable report on the curative powers of the water at the Grotto, but the most reliable analyses quickly proved that it was ordinary water. Later, some wanted to attribute special radiations to Lourdes, Medjugorje and other sanctuaries, but this has never been seriously confirmed.

We must see these phenomena for what they are. Today as yesterday, symbolism and sensationalism are constant factors of popular phenomena, whether religious or not. The press, to a great extent, brings to the fore events, persons, and things of current interest. It makes them the subject of make-believe, a locus predisposed for dreams at night, and special forces by day. In this way it mobilizes public opinion and gives rise to crowds that come in pilgrimage. In an age of demytholigization, new myths have seen a development without precedent.

Man has need of simplification to be at ease in a life that is more and more complicated. He readily gives material form to his attachments. In their wallets, many keep a photo, a cherished letter. These little rituals of their personal life support their attachments and keep them from forgetting. The rigidity of an intellectual criticism, so dear to certain theologians, too often brings about boredom, aversion and a suffocation of a faith without religion, without bonds. Man is a material being who lives in an environment of the senses. It is useless to try to tear him from it. He needs symbols, signs and gestures.

As an intellectual, I was for a long time offended by the fact that pilgrims kissed the rock when going through the grotto at Lourdes. The rock is nothing, but they do this readily, in memory of the act of penance demanded of Bernadette: "Kiss the earth in penance for sinners." This had appalled those who witnessed it on February 25, 1858 (the day that Bernadette discovered the spring). This gesture, this act of penance, has been perpetuated in a more refined form. One no longer gets down on the ground to kiss the earth, but standing up kisses the wall of rock. That same day, Bernadette also ate a bitter herb which grew in the grotto. This action shocked people even more and for a long time. The judges, both civil and ecclesiastical reproached her:

"You ate grass like the beasts," they said to her.

"You eat salad readily enough," she answered.

This surprising ritual has not been kept up at Lourdes. Otherwise it would have been necessary to cultivate the herb commercially. In 1958 there were only one or two tufts of it at the grotto.

Care must be taken that the gestures and rituals of pilgrimages do not become superstition. Lourdes is very strict about this. Chaplains forbid the Italian pilgrims there to brandish their candles while singing the *Ave Maria.* Some ask whether this repression does not go too far. Others reproach charismatics for raising their arms towards Heaven when they pray.

MAGIC PROPERTIES ATTRIBUTED TO RELICS

Particularly criticized is the importance given to the bodies of saints—the goal of numerous pilgrimages.

"An inheritance from paganism," some complain.

It has not been sufficiently noted that the ordinary goal of these pilgrimages is not so much the *body* as the *tomb.* The body is no longer in the tomb of Christ at Jerusalem. It is the Resurrection to which the empty tomb gives witness, and the name Resurrection was given to the shrines from the very first.

Pilgrims have been reproached for attributing to the bodies of saints mysterious properties: radiant energy for example. People wonder about this text of Theodoret of Cyr regarding the dividing up of relics:

"In a body that is divided up (if it is parcelled out to distribute relics), grace remains undivided and the fragments, however small they may be, keep the same power as the entire body" (Sermon 8, pg. 83, 1011; *Sources chrétiennes* 57, 314).

But this same Theodoret of Cyr insists, above all, on the relative importance of saints' bodies. If he exalts their triumph and underlines that this body was the living temple of God, he also points out that their cult signifies something entirely different:

"No, pilgrims do not resort to them as to some gods, but they invoke them as people of God, and they pray to them that they act as their ambassadors [. . .]. The ex-votos, which attest to cures [. . .] proclaim the power of the martyrs who repose there, and this power certainly shows that their God is the true God" (ib. p. 83, 1932; *Sources chrétiennes* 57, 333-334).

Such is the constant teaching of the Church:

"It is God who is honored through the relics of the saints [. . .]. It is more valuable to imitate in one's heart their examples than to carry their bones suspended around one's neck," said Alcuin (9th century), cited by J. Chelini (p. 122).

"What madman would dare maintain that the bodies of the saints ought not to receive our veneration here below, since it is God whom we

adore in His dear servants, whose prayers help
us to gain Heaven? Peter is not God, but I hope
to be freed from my sin through the prayers of
Peter," as Ernold Le Noir says in a similar way
(Text cited, ib. 122).

The respect given to the bodies of the saints hinges on
the fact that they were temples of God and that they await
the resurrection for a future life. Anything else is excess
and superfluity. There has been some of that in the veneration of relics.

The apparently excessive prominence given to certain
features held in honor at pilgrimages (images, grottos,
springs) must not be caricatured. In a nation that is alive,
the flag and other memorials are held in honor and
induce men to give their lives for their country without
attributing an intrinsic power to these symbols.

Christianity has often done harm in baptizing, that is,
in purifying, reorienting, performing ceremonies and
making pilgrimages that originate at pagan sites. But then
too, this is often done in an irreproachable way as at
Gudalupe, where Our Lady appeared on the site of the
cruel goddess Tonantzin to eliminate and supplant her.

Abuses in the matter of relics have now been overcome
and are forgotten. Let us leave the dead to bury the dead.

COMMERCIALISM

Today one of the complaints most frequently heard is
the commercialism of pilgrimages. It is a fact that the
influx of millions of persons brings on the marketing of
millions of pious objects.

The Eiffel Tower, the pyramids of Egypt and many
other tourist sites, prompt the manufacture of souvenirs
in great numbers. We do not inhibit commerce which has
a role in human life. The souvenir is not necessarily fetish-
ism, and all the commercial articles created for this purpose are not bad. The pastoral at Lourdes has found a
way to combat and eliminate the most offensive Lourdes

stone (that makes men virile) and to direct the industries dealing with pious objects towards models that are proper and even edifying, which pilgrims, moreover, will wisely prefer to the other kinds.

VAIN ATTACHMENT TO PLACES

Theologically speaking, the most serious objection remains: Why run to distant shrines, since the New Testament knows nothing of them and since the presence of Christ in the Eucharist is accessible everywhere, and is all we need?

The reason for a Christian pilgrimage is not an encounter (with God) in a particular spot, for this encounter takes place everywhere, as Jesus taught in *John* 4:23. But the pilgrimage has the value of a symbol and of an action. It deepens the possibilities for an encounter within the human heart, on the wings of dreams that make up one third of a person's life (the time given to sleep) and orients the other two thirds. One may not shortcircuit this dimension.

This is why a pilgrimage is first of all detachment, penance, a tearing oneself from a profane milieu and from sin, but also an impetus towards God alone, with the vital forces of body and soul. In a remarkable way, a pilgrimage brings together the visual and auditory, the physical and spiritual faculties to set in motion a quest for an interior cure and sometimes a bodily one (the latter being a symbol of the former) and for a special encounter with God.

Historians and sociologists define a pilgrimage by way of its sacred end. Sociologically, the sacred would be the beneficent radiance that cures and converts. Such is the attraction of a pilgrimage. But for the Christian, the sacred is identified with Christ, God became man, who died for the love of mankind. If then pilgrimages have a reason for being, it is that they liberate us, detach us from what shackles us and creates in our heart a place of welcome for Christ. This explains why the Eucharist takes an ever larger place in Christian pilgrimages. The pastoral work of pilgrimages creates and defines the goal of a journey upon what is essential: the Lord Himself.

The history of pilgrimages is traversed by a tension between magic, that wishes to acquire a beneficent power through some technique, and the sacred, which is centered on adoration and the workings of grace, which is more properly religious. But adoration does not exclude the humble request for God's freely given blessings, which come from His wisdom and love.

THE PILGRIMAGE OF LIFE

If according to current thinking, a pilgrimage is a journey, limited to time, this journey, theologically speaking, has meaning in the life of each Christian and of the Church itself. The New Testament considers both as on a pilgrimage.

It is essentially the life of the Church, which Scripture presents as an Exodus led by the Lord Jesus (*Acts* 3:15; 5:31; *Heb.* 2:10), and as an eschatological pilgrimage (*2 Cor.* 5:6 ff.; *Heb.* 13:14).

This theology of pilgrimage is developed between two poles. At the point of departure, Christians are born of God through their baptism. Thenceforth they are "not of this world" (*John* 17:16). They have "no lasting city here below." They live in exile (*1 Peter* 1:17), travelers on the earth (*1 Peter* 11 and *Heb.* 11:13).

The pilgrimage of the Christian life is characterized by courage, hope, patience and perseverance in journeying toward repose in God, symbol of holiness itself. The end is the Heavenly Jerusalem (*Rev.* 21), where God, the All in All, is the sole and true light.

Vatican II revived this biblical and traditional theme in the Constitution on the Church, *(Lumen Gentium)*, the Council's fundamental text:

> The Church goes forward in pilgrimage in the midst of persecutions from the world and the consolations of God (St. Augustine, *City of God*

18, 51, 2; PL 46, 614). She proclaims the cross
and the death of the Lord until He comes (no.
8 and 4).

In the chapter on the people of God, which restructures
all of ecclesiology, the Council resumes the theme from
scriptural sources:

> Just as Israel according to the flesh, which
> journeyed in pilgrimage through the desert was
> already called the Church of God, so too the
> new Israel which goes forward in the present
> age, in quest of the future city (*Heb.* 13:14) is
> also called the Church of Christ (*Matt.* 16:18)
> redeemed by His blood (*Acts* 20:28) and filled
> with the Holy Spirit.
> [...]. Throughout human history, she
> marches through trials and tribulations, upheld
> by the power of the grace of God, promised to
> her [...] that she be renewed constantly under
> the action of the Holy Spirit (LG no. 9 and 3).

The third Eucharistic prayer of the Mass invokes God,
asking that He vivify this pilgrimage, inherent in the history of salvation:
"Strengthen in faith and love your pilgrim Church on
earth."
If the life of each Christian and the life of the Church
are, according to Scripture and tradition, a pilgrimage, it
will not be surprising that Mary, prototype of the Church
and of each Christian, would be an integral part of this
venture.

MARY, MODEL, INSPIRATION AND
OBJECT OF PILGRIMAGES

Such are the fundamental biblical, theological, and
spiritual concepts concerning pilgrimages. We come now
to the specific object of this work, the place of Mary in

and practice of pilgrimages.

.s an important place under several titles: as
..i, as inspiration, and as object of pilgrimages, and
as model of the Christian journey in the totality of her
life, prototype of the pilgrimage of the Church itself.

MARY, MODEL OF PILGRIMS

Mary took part regularly in the traditional pilgrimages
of her people to the one sanctuary, the Temple of
Jerusalem.

The Visitation is certainly a pilgrimage: Mary, who
became the sanctuary of the Son of God incarnate (*Luke*
1:28-35), goes to her cousin Elizabeth, beneficiary of a
similar and a related grace, not only to share this grace,
but drawn also by Jerusalem (*Luke* 1:39-56). Elizabeth
was the wife of a priest of the Temple, living in the
suburbs of the holy city (Ain Karem according to tradition). During the three months that she spent with her
cousin, Mary would not have neglected to frequent the
Temple. She and her cousin brought their prayer there
(*Luke* 1:29-56).

Her first pilgrimage to the Temple that is formally
reported by Scripture is the one she made forty days after
the birth of Jesus, for the "purification," according to
Luke 2:22-35. But the Evangelist changes this rite of the
purification of the mother after childbirth, into a purification of the Temple, to signify that the Lord Jesus (*Luke*
2:7) entering the Temple, so long deprived of the Ark of
the Covenant and of the Shekinah, purifies his priests and
his people (R. Laurentin, *The Truth of Christmas, Beyond
the Myths,* St. Bede's Publications, 1986, p. 193-207).

Mary also made the annual pilgrimage to Jerusalem
despite the distance from Nazareth in Galilee. It was a
place far from the center of things, situated more than
a hundred kilometers away, along rugged winding roads,
beset by brigands.

That Mary regularly made this pilgrimage every year
(*Luke* 2:41) explains why we find her in Jerusalem at the

Passover, at the time of the death of Christ, in April of the year 30 (*John* 19:25-27; *Acts* 1:14). This brings up the question: Where did she celebrate the Paschal meal, that family ceremony? It would normally be with Jesus, but the Gospel gives no detail either to confirm or deny this hypothesis. All the same, *Luke* 8:1-3 leads us to think that the women disciples who "were with Him" on the roads, were present there just as the Twelve were. Why would they have been excluded that evening?

Mary, voluntarily a virgin, was also a pilgrim voluntarily, for the law obliged only men to make the annual pilgrimage. Her assiduity is therefore significant.

SHE WHO INSPIRES

Does Mary instill the spirit of pilgrimages? *Luke* 2:44 enables us to glimpse the influence of she who was full of grace. The perfect prayer of the Immaculate radiated, as all true prayers radiate, with a profundity that is hard to imagine. Mary, imbued with the psalms as is manifest in her canticle of the Magnificat, filled with classic expressions and reminiscences, was at ease with this kind of prayer.

It is clear that she made this pilgrimage in spirit and in truth, not in the way that the prophets criticized when they said: *"I detest, I despise your pilgrimages,"* says Jahweh. *"There is nothing in your offerings that pleases me"* (*Amos* 5:21-27).

With the caravan along the road, she probably sang the Gradual Psalms (*Psalms* 120-134), which express the attachment of the pilgrims to the house of the Lord and to the Holy City. She had for the Temple that love that she instilled in Jesus and which is summed up in this dictum from *Psalm* 69:10, and taken up again in *John* 2:17: *"Zeal for your house consumes me."*

This enthusiasm for the house of the Father (*Luke* 2:48) had an eschatological dimension nourished by the prophets. For them, pilgrimages were a rough plan and prefiguration of the pilgrimage of the end times, when the people of Israel and the pagans would finally be reunited. At the Presentation in the Temple, Mary brought only the offering of the poor. All the more, then, is she the model for that "little remnant" of God (*Jer.* 40:11).

MARY AND THE REMNANT OF ISRAEL

This term "remnant" has had quite a history, beginning with a prehistory. The punishments of Israel in the desert cause a significant part of the people to disappear (*Ex.* 32:38; *Num.* 17:14; 21:6; 25:9).

The idea takes on a growing spiritual importance even before the exile. According to Isaiah, "the remnant" will participate in the holiness of Yahweh (*Is.* 4:3; cf. 6:3). He will be a destroyer for the impious, but for the others a luminous flame (10:17), and a purifying one (1:25-28). This "remnant," a work of Yahweh (4:4) will rely on God alone (10:20). It is made up principally of the poor (14:32). It will rally around the Messiah (10:21), who will be its head and its glory (4:2).

Beginning with the exile, the "remnant" appears as a religious elite within the people: the "faithful remnant" (*Rom.* 11:5). It is Israel, the servant of God, Israel *"in which I shall be glorified"* says God (*Is.* 49:3). It is given a mission with respect to all of Israel.

After the exile, the small community of the exiles returned to Sion call themselves "the remnant." They are only the seed of the restoration and of the eschatological promises (*Hosea* 2:23 ff., *Ez.* 34:26 ff.). Finally the people of God are identified with the poor of Yahweh (*Is.* 49:13; *Ps.* 18:28; 149:4).

Mary is placed at the head of the poor (*Luke* 1:48 and 52), somewhat as Abraham is at the head of the people of God. Abraham is the original historical personification, and Mary the final personification, proclaimed blessed by all generations because the Lord has regarded her lowlines and has done great things for her (*Luke* 1:48-49). Greatness with respect to God, and human littleness, characterize Mary.

The theology of the poor and of the "remnant" is inseparable from the eschatological dynamism of prophetic theology. Mary then anticipates and makes her own the attitude set forth in *Hebrews* 9:11-12. Her prayer went beyond the walls of the Temple then under construction: *"through the greater and more perfect tabernacle, not made by hands."*

This eschatological perspective does not diminish the concrete, physical and spiritual devotion Mary had for the Temple of God.

Very early on, Christians dedicated their basilicas and churches to the Mother of God, the first dwelling of the Lord. Many churches, cathedrals and shrines thus dedicated to Mary, have become privileged places of pilgrimage. Similarly, the places associated with her life, above all those of the Incarnation (Nazareth and Bethlehem).

MARY'S LIFE AS A PILGRIMAGE

Finally, Mary's entire life is an exemplary pilgrimage, from her Immaculate Conception, a perfect and dynamic point of departure, to her Assumption. This last involved not only her soul but also her body. Hers was then an integral pilgrimage. It saw the crowning of the dramatic stages sown with trials, notably the following:

— The virginal conception created a threatening situation not only with respect to Joseph (whom Heaven forewarned), but also with respect to the family clan of Nazareth. Mary ran the danger not only out of public censure, but of being stoned.

— The departure for Bethlehem, in conditions that were especially precarious and wearying, being on the point of giving birth (*Luke* 2:1-7). Perhaps this was a means of avoiding the suspicions and gossip of the village, which would have been surprised at this birth six months after entering the house of Joseph.

— The threat of Herod and the flight to Egypt (*Matt.* 2:13-15).

— The problems of returning and of resettlement (*Matt.* 2:19-23).
— The trials of daily life at a time and in an underdeveloped country with its chronic famines.
— The death of Joseph, and then the departure of Jesus, which left her all alone.
— The mobilizing of the clan which involved Mary in its effort to turn Jesus away from his prophetic fancies (*Mark* 3:21, 31-35).
— The drama of the passion and death of Jesus.
— His definitive departure after the Ascension.
— Tensions in the primitive community of Jerusalem, where she lived according to *Acts* 1:14.
— Persecutions and difficulties, relative to the care of widows among whom she was numbered (*Acts* 6:1-6).

The Assumption is the eschatological icon of her earthly pilgrimage, the entrance of the Ark of the Covenant into the heavenly Jerusalem, where she rejoined Christ with her glorified body (whether through death or not), for a complete communion with God in Jesus Christ. She is the exemplary prototype of our resurrection, and the definitive outcome of our own earthly pilgrimage.

PART III

CHAPTER 1

Sanctuaries (or Shrines)

Today, sanctuaries are one of the most visible aspects of the Church, to the point that this word designates both the community of Christians and the building that unites them. However, the history of shrines is very complex and full of incident. They appeared, slowly, not without misgivings, and with unexpected and significant disappearances.

In English, as in French, the word "sanctuary" comes from the Latin *sanctus,* (holy), and signifies a holy place, separated from the realm of the profane, elevated above and belonging to God, referring to Him alone, according to His invitation:
— *"Be holy as I am holy."*
In the New Testament, we find many synonymous expressions, which are translated by "sanctuary" or "temple."
Church (Greek, *ecclesia*) designates a people, called, brought together. In the Old and New Testaments, this word indicates a religious assembly as well as a political one.
Let us note that the word *Ecclesia* is absent from the Gospels except in *Matthew,* Chapters 16 and 18. Jesus speaks more readily of "reign" and "kingdom" (dynamic

45

terms), than of Church. This term emerges only in the foundational texts, having a juridical and institutional significance, such as Peter's office, and the correction or excommunication of sinners.

THE BEGINNING OF SANCTUARIES (SHRINES)

1. The Nomadic Period: before Sanctuaries (2000-1250 B.C.)

In the Bible there are no sanctuaries at the beginning. According to *Genesis,* man was created in the garden of paradise, and there without any building, ritual, or cultic object, he encountered God *"in the cool of the day"* (*Gen.* 3:8).

There is no building either in the book of *Genesis* or in the book of *Exodus.* There are only places where God showed Himself to His elect, beginning with the patriarchs. They commemorated Him, sometimes with a stele or an improvised memorial, not with a temple. Exegetes are inclined to think that these memorials of the patriarchs, conjured up to explain the origin of the cultic places in Israel, are only late attempts to integrate into Yahwism the cultic places of the Canaanites or others, adopted by the people dispersed at the time of the Judges.

The nomadic sanctuaries of the Ark of the Covenant then began to appear.

On Sinai, Moses inaugurated a place of worship. God accompanied His nomad people, beneath the tent of the Covenant, like the one of the Israelites in the *Exodus.* God's ascendency established the sacred character of the Ark and of the Tent (also called the Tabernacle). According to *Exodus,* God Himself consecrated this first sanctuary, and showed it by two signs:

— the cloud, "above," which signifies the transcendence of His presence,
— and the glory radiating "from within" the Ark, which signifies His presence in the midst of His people.

2. Sanctuaries in the Holy Land (1200 to 1000 B.C.)

In the anarchic period which followed the conquest of the promised land, after the death of Joshua, the people established or adapted a number of sacred places, or sanctuaries, that are mentioned in the Bible: *Joshua, Judges, 1-2 Samuel,* and *1-2 Kings;* notably in 1 *Samuel* 7, 15-17:

> *Samuel judged Israel as long as he lived. He made a yearly journey, passing through Bethel, Gilgal and Mizpah and judging Israel at each of these sanctuaries. Then he used to return to Ramah, for that was his home. There, too, he judged Israel and built an altar to the Lord.*

Let us situate the sanctuaries thus enumerated and some others:

Bethel fittingly enough signified House of God. This city is situated seventeen kilometers north of Jerusalem, on the road to Sichem (*Jgs.* 20:31). Its Canaanite name was Luz. There was a sacred tree there (*Gen.* 35:8) and a sanctuary where the god Bethel was worshipped (*Jer.* 48:13). It was the Israelites who gave to Luz the name of "Bethel" and it was there that Abraham discovered the land that God was giving him. (*Gen.* 13:14). And it was there that the son of Abraham saw in a dream the "ladder of Jacob" (cf. 35, 1-15). It was one of the first cities conquered by Joshua. People came to Bethel to consult God or to meet the judges. In the ninth century, the city became the center for a brotherhood of prophets grouped around Elias and Eliseus.

Gilgal, whose name means a circle of stones, was situated between the Jordan and Jericho, probably northeast of that city. It was the first encampment of the Israelites at their entrance into Canaan, after crossing the Jordan. There Joshua celebrated the Passover and was favored with a vision. It was there that he concluded a terrestrial alliance with the Gabaonites and was the point of departure for the conquest of Canaan. It was the principal sanctuary of the tribe of Benjamin and where Saul was proclaimed king (*1 Sam.* 11:14-15), and then rejected by Samuel. But worship at Gilgal, no doubt contaminated by Canaanite customs, was condemned by the prophets, once the unity of the one sanctuary was established (*Hosea* 4:15).

Mizpah is a city of Benjamin (*Joshua* 18:26). It was a traditional center for the gathering together of Israel. At the time of Samuel, the people there fasted and offered a libation, while Samuel offered a sacrifice (*1 Sam.* 7:5-12, 16). It was there that Saul was chosen king.

Schechem, city of Mount Ephraim at the entrance to the gorge between Mount Ebal and Mount Garizim, was a place of communication between Jerusalem and Phoenicia (Jordan and the Mediterranian). It was a holy place associated with the patriarchs. There was venerated the oak of Mamre, where God appeared (*Gen.* 12:6-7; 35:4). There Jacob purchased a field from the sons of "Hamor, founder of Schechem" (*Gen.* 33: 18-19). Joseph was buried there (*Joshua* 24:32). It was a city of refuge (*Joshua* 20:7), given to the Levites of the clan of Kohath and was for a time the seat for the Ark (Jos. 8:33) placed there where the Canaanites worshipped their god of the covenant Baal.

3. The Ark enters Israel (ca. 1200 to 1000 B.C.)

The Ark of the Covenant had found a home at Gilgal, Shechem, Bethel, and then Shilo, the last location of this sanctuary before Jerusalem.

Shilo, the last stopping place, was situated in the land of Canaan. It was the site of a sanctuary and it was there that the parents of Samuel had a son and gave him back to that holy place (*1 Sam.* 1-3). Samuel slept in the sanctuary, near the Ark of the Covenant. And it was there that he received his vocation. It is of little importance to us what the city became after it was destroyed, no doubt by the Philistines. Shiloh remained a traditional sanctuary after the departure of the Ark, but the people of Shiloh went readily on pilgrimage to Jerusalem. Today the city is called Khirbet Seilum.

The last resting place of the Ark was the most disturbed. The Philistines captured it (*1 Sam.* 4:11), but epidemics and plagues terrorized the cities where the Ark was taken (*1 Sam.* 5). At the end of seven months, they returned it with lavish ritual reparations. It remained there for twenty years, when Samuel transferred it to Mizpah to clear out the worship of the Baals and the Astartes (*1 Sam.* 7:4). There people fasted and made reparation for these idolatries. An attack by the Philistines was victoriously repulsed.

4. The Ark in Jerusalem (ca. 1000 B.C.)

After the reign of Saul, David conquered Jerusalem and brought the Ark there. David and all the house of Israel danced before Jahweh with all their might and sang with lyres, etc. (*2 Sam.* 6:5). He had the Ark stay at the home of Obed-Edom, of Gat, a Philistine whom *1 Chronicles* 16:38 will make a Levite. But his house is blessed (contrary to what happened to the Philistines or to Uzzah, who were punished). From there the transfer continues:

David, girt with a linen apron, came dancing before the Lord with abandon (*2 Sam.* 6:13:14).

Michal, Saul's daughter, was shocked and despised the king for having thus revealed his nakedness, something not in keeping with his dignity. But her lack of comprehension for David's zeal for Yahweh will be punished: she would be sterile until her death.

Upon arriving in Jerusalem, David deposits the Ark beneath its tent (always a tent, as in the desert). The king, then being the chief priest, David:

> *offered holocausts and peace offerings before the Lord. When he finished making these offerings, he blessed the people in the name of the Lord of Hosts. He then distributed among the people* (*2 Sam.* 6: 17-19).

5. The Temple (ca. 970 B.C.)

For God and for his Ark, David wanted to build an edifice not less sumptious than his own dwelling, but the prophet Nathan made him understand that this construction would be the work of the son who would succeed him on his throne. The reason for this pronouncement is revealed later.

> *You have shed much blood, and you have waged great wars. You may not build a house in my honor because you have shed too much blood upon the earth in my sight. However, a son is to be born to you. He will be a peaceful man...for Solomon will be his name. In his time I will bestow peace and tranquility on Israel. It is he who shall build a house in my honor; he shall be a son to me, and I will be a father to him, etc. (1 Chr. 22: 8-10).*

Solomon then built a magnificent Temple (*1 Kgs.* 5-8) in the fourth year of his reign. The transfer of the Ark and the dedication of the Temple were a grandiose celebration. King Solomon, still the leading religious figure before the installation of a specialized priesthood, celebrated the sacrifice as high priest and blessed the people (*2 Chr.* 6:3; *1 Kings* 8:14).

It was after this that the priesthood was organized for service in the Temple. It would take on a growing importance, and, according to the priestly document, the High Priest was to receive a consecration and royal insignia (*Ex.* 28:29; *Lev.* 8-9). Thus began the long history of the tensions between the kings and the priests. (The popes eventually took over the title of Sovereign Pontiff, which originally belonged to the Roman Emperor.)

The two-fold importance of the Ark of the Covenant and of the royal capital gave the sanctuary of Jerusalem an incomparable preeminence.

But a tension persisted between the sanctuary of Yahweh

and so many other sanctuaries that were in various degrees of an idolatrous character. This idolatry has a long history, for the descendants of Abraham adored, in addition to Yahweh, some strange gods. They allowed themselves to be led into honoring Canaanite gods, and then later, Assyrian and Babylonian divinities (*1 Kgs.* 14: 22-24; *2 Kgs.* 21:2-9; *Hosea* 2:8-13).

Several Israelite kings practiced idolatry, even in Jerusalem, under the influence of their foreign wives, beginning with Solomon!

> *When Solomon was old, his wives had turned his heart to strange gods; and his heart was not wholly with Yahweh his God as his father David's had been. Solomon became a follower of Astarte, the goddess of the Sidonians and of Milcom, the Ammonite abomination (...). He built a high place on the mountain to the east of Jerusalem for Chemosh, the abomination of Moab, and to Milcom, the abomination of the Amonnites. He did the same for all his foreign wives, etc. (1 Kgs. 11:3-13).*

6. The Temple of Jerusalem: the only sanctuary

The Ark of the Covenant was, more than a constitutional law would have been, the charter and the sacred foundation of the nation. Its enthronement made Jerusalem a sacred religious capital at the same time as a military and political one.

But the cult of Yahweh competed with the Canaanite cults. The kings and their wives exemplified this syncretism, caught in the toils of local nature worship, rooted in the earth and local culture.

Josias (640-609 B.C.), the sixteenth king of Juda, accomplished the most important reform in the time of the kings. He renewed the Covenant and celebrated a solemn Passover in Jerusalem (*2 Kgs.* 23, *2 Chr.* 34).

> *Then Josias commanded [that there be removed] from the sanctuary of Yahweh all the objects that had been made for Baal, Ashera, and the whole host of heaven. He had these burned outside Jerusalem [...] and he put an end to the pseudo-priests whom the kings of Judah had appointed to offer sacrifice on the high places [...] and in the neighborhood of Jerusalem and those who sacrificed to Baal, to the sun, the moon, the constellations and the whole array of heaven. And from the Temple of Yahweh, he took the sacred pole outside Jerusalem and in the Kedron valley he burnt it, etc. (2 Kgs. 23:4-6).*

From then on the law prescribed the pilgrimage to Jerusalem:
— Three times a year all your menfolk must appear before Yahweh in the place chosen by him.
— at the feast of Unleavened Bread,
— at the feast of Weeks,
— at the feast of Shelters (Booths).
— No one must appear empty-handed before Yahweh. Each must give what he can, in proportion to the blessing which Yahweh your God has bestowed on you (*Deut.* 16:16-17; *Ex.* 23:14-17).

7. The Deportation and the Destruction of the Temple.
After the death of Josias (609 B.C.), Jerusalem was besieged, fell; and Jehoiakim (598-597) was deported to Babylon. Ten years later, after the brief reign of Zedekiah, son of Josias (597-587), Jerusalem was retaken. The Temple had been burned, and there was another deportation. It was at this time that the Ark finally disappeared (2 Kgs. 25).

During the exile in Babylon, religious purity grew more intense. The trial became a great moment for conversion and spiritual enlightenment.

8. The Sacred Temple.

In 538, the deportees, freed by an edict of Cyrus, returned to Palestine and built the second Temple, whose dedication was celebrated in 515.

The Temple was rebuilt with the assistance of the Sidonians and the Syrians, who furnished wood and the "cedars of Lebanon" (*Ezra* 1:6; *Haggai* 1:14-15). This temple was more modest than the preceding one but a portico was joined to it.

9. The Critical Spirit of the Prophets.

We cannot overstress how strongly the prophets denounced the equivocal character of the Temple contaminated by:
— the idolatrous worship of the kings and their wives.
— the formalism of the priests.

They criticized ritual worship, favoring a true, sincere worship coming from the heart and extending to all of life, including social justice and aid to the poor (*Is.* 58:1-14). They went so far as to prophesy (and so anticipated Jesus) the destruction of the Temple, in punishment for the sin of the nation. Here as elsewhere, they prepared and anticipated the Gospel in a surprising way.

Despite the radical nature of these expressions, it is not worship that they were fighting against, but its formalism. They criticized the exterior because they wished to restore the worship of Yahweh, without which all the rest is nothing. Beyond the sacrifices of animals is the sacrifice of the heart: a pure heart (*Ps.* 51:12), a broken, contrite heart (*Ps.* 51:17), a new heart created by God (*Jer.* 31:33).

The exile, far from the Temple, created a profound movement for spiritual worship in accord with that interior religion of the *heart,* preached by *Deuteronomy* (6:45 ff., where this word occurs some fifty times and more than a hundred times in the *Psalms*), and in *Jeremiah* (31:33). In the land of exile, people already understood that God is present everywhere, that He reigns everywhere, and is adored everywhere (*Ez.* 11:16). His glory was not manifested to Ezechiel, captive in pagan Babylon. For this reason, at the end of the exile, certain prophets put those repatriated on guard against an excessive attachment to the temple of stone:

> *Thus says Yahweh:*
> *With Heaven my throne*
> *and earth my footstool,*
> *what home could you build me? [. . .]*
> *But my eyes are drawn to the person*
> *of humbled and contrite spirit [. . .]*
> 　　　　　　　　　　　　　(*Is.* 66:1-3)

One can sense a tension between the priestly milieux who reform, strengthen, and restructure the priesthood during the exile, and the prophets who insist on the spirit, without contesting the priesthood and the rituals established as such. They simply wish to redefine the interior.

Finally, the second Temple was profaned and pillaged in 169 B.C. Pagans offered sacrifices there to the god Zeus, on the altar of holocausts. But the temple was purified and reconsecrated in 164, thanks to Judas Macchabeus (*1 Mac.* 4:36).

10. The Third Temple finished in 28 A.D.

The third Temple was built by Herod the Great. This was a political move to insure the support of the priests. This Temple is known from descriptions by Flavius Josephus (*Jewish Antiquities* and *The Jewish Wars*). It took forty-six years to rebuild this Temple (*John* 2:30), whose ruin Jesus predicted. Excavations and research, conducted over ten years, starting in 1968 by P. Mazard, have improved our knowledge of this building, so frequently visited by Jesus.

11. From the Temple to Christian Worship (30-70 A.D.).

As per the example of Christ, who as a pious layman practiced all the rituals of the Jewish religion, Christians also frequented the Temple (*Acts* 2:46; 3:1-8). They all remained *"staunch upholders of the law" (Acts* 21:20). But they already had their own specific form of worship: "the breaking of bread." It was a private, domestic worship, that took place at the home (*Col.* 4:15) of one of the Christians, chosen for its adequate size and the hospitable character of the master of the house.

However, persecutions gradually separated the Christians from the Temple, where the Apostles were very soon arrested and imprisoned (*Acts* 4-5). Persecution, which essentially targeted preachers and prophets (*Acts* 7), barred them from the Temple, which was completely destroyed for the last time in the year 70, by Roman troops under Titus. The last attempts at reconstruction, notably by Simeon, Bar-Kokba (132-135), were never finished. There remains only the west wall, along which the Jews of Jerusalem come to pray today.

Christian worship being of a domestic and unobtrusive character, has left few traces. There are no archeological remains and only a few texts (*Col.* 4:15), and the continual reference to the homes of Christians who received the Eucharist (*Rom.* 16:10-11; *Phil.* 4:22; *Col.* 4:15).

When a Christian community grew in size, it was no doubt necessary, we can suppose, to acquire a place large enough for its needs. But history does not know all the solutions adopted during the first and second centuries.

According to Eusebius, however, cities where Christianity had been implanted possessed house churches from the third century (*Ecclesiastical History* 8:1, 2; Pg. 20).

Some have thought that house churches of the first centuries were of the type seen at Pompei. It is possible that they were of that style, but this is a supposition that remains without proof, inasmuch as the Pompeian house was practically unknown in the large cities of the third century. What does appear certain is that from the middle of the third century, in the East and in Africa, Christian communities began to build meeting places.

In the third century, when the Greeks speak of the "House of the Lord" (*Oikia Kuriake*), or when the Latins speak of the *Domus Domini*, they no doubt mean the place for the Eucharistic liturgy.

In the house church, the principal room, set aside for celebrating the liturgy, acquired, ipso facto, a sacred character. But the celebration of Eucharistic worship sufficed to consecrate it.

Archaeology has greatly demythologized the notion of worship in the catacombs (cf. the novel *Fabiola*), for the primitive galleries there were only narrow corridors (ordinarily only a meter wide), which scarcely lent themselves to gathering an assembly together. The chambers with their sarcophagi and their *loculi* (coffins?) could serve small groups of intimates for the funeral meals that were then widespread. The Eucharist could then be celebrated there, but there is no proof that these places were churches of refuge. The secret character of Christian cemeteries, moreover, is merely a myth, for the catacombs were places officially declared to be such. The cadastral survey had the plans, the city administration knew the names of the proprieters, and in a period of crisis, they were confiscated like all the other properties of the Church, notably under Valerian in 257 and under Diocletian in 303. It was only in the fourth century that certain cemeteries were greatly transformed and became something like underground basilicas. Victorious Christianity exalted its martyrs. The catacombs were rather places where one evoked the memory of the dead.

12. Constantinian Basilicas.

The conversion of the Emperor Constantine, after his victory at the Milvian Bridge on 28 October 312, gave freedom of worship to the endangered Christians. From that time on, they built places of worship adopting the plan of the basilica, which signifies a royal edifice, from the Greek *basileus,* meaning king. At Rome, in Jerusalem, Bethlehem and Byzantium, Constantine himself had some sumptious buildings erected on this model. Such is the Constantinian church of the Nativity in Bethlehem. Archaeology has discovered many Christian basilicas built during the fourth, fifth and sixth centuries, while at the same time the ancient places of worship, which had remained inconspicuous because of persecutions, were enlarged or tranformed. It was then that the Church, now become visible, systematically incorporated into its worship the sacralizing rites of the Old Testament. Thus there was inaugurated the consecration of churches and basilicas by the bishop. This ritualizing did not take place without the danger of a return to formalism.

13. Taking over the Pagan Temples.

Some pagan temples also became churches, but rather late, for Constantine, who remained royal pontiff of the traditional religion, did not deprive paganism of its places of worship. Besides, Christians were revolted at setting themselves up in those places of idolatrous abominations. Temples were alternatively closed, reopened, demolished, rebuilt. They were turned over to the Christians only in the last years of the fourth century. The earliest cases known were at Damascus and Hieropolis in 389, Egypt in 390, and then elsewhere.

This was the case in Sicily for eight temples that were converted and dedicated to the Blessed Virgin in 431, according to Beugnot *Histoire de la destruction du paganisme en Occident,* Paris, 1835, v. 2, p. 271). In Milan, the temples of Minerva, Janus, Hercules and Apollo, likewise became Christian sanctuaries (DACL 11, article Milan). In Rome, this happened to two temples close to each other. In the sixth century, under Felix IV, the Pantheon became the Church of the Blessed Virgin and all the Martyrs; the other one, under Boniface IV, in the seventh century, became the Basilica of Saints Cosmas and Damian. Other examples are cited in the Catholic Encyclopedia.

According to doctrine, it is not the building and the cement that are important. The temple of God, from now on, is the Christian. Each of them is consecrated by the Sacrament of Baptism and so is their communitarian gathering, according to the word of Christ:

> *Where two or three are gathered in my name, there am I in their midst* (*Matt.* 18:20).

According to the theology of the New Testament, what is sacred are persons and their life, which God divinizes and calls to eternal life in communion with Him. The objects and instruments of worship are only signs, blessed or consecrated for the good use that Christians and Christian assemblies will make of them.

In its entirety, this history is that of a double drama: to free the worship of the true God from faulty unions and ambient syncretisms, so widely prevalent in our own day and too confusedly ecumenical, and from the formalism which often follows upon the development and standardization of mere ritual forms.

It is important, above all, to situate the radical change in the history of revealed religion that Christ introduced, not in a theoretical, but in a vital way.

CHAPTER 2

The Meaning of This Evolution

TEMPLE, PRIESTHOOD AND SACRIFICE, TRANSFERRED TO JESUS CHRIST ALONE

The cultic development realized in Jesus Christ is His replacing of the Temple, the priesthood and the sacrifices of the Old Testament. All has been fulfilled in Him. This radical change appears rather like a revolution than an evolution. As regards worship, how are we to understand the words of Christ: "I have not come to abolish but to fulfill," for despite the strict observance of the law by Jesus Himself, and by the first Christians, we see in the middle of the first century the abolition of the Temple, the priesthood and of the ancient sacrifices of the Old Testament.

The essential consists in this: in the Old Testament, the Temple, priesthood, and sacrifice were ritual figures, gradually codified and specified: a building, a hereditary caste, and the offering of immolated animals as sacrifices. In Jesus Christ, the reality takes the place of the figures. It is unified in a plan clearly traced by the prophets. In a word, the temple, the priesthood and the sacrifice are accomplished in Jesus Christ. He is henceforth the only Temple, the sole Priest, and the unique sacrifice. He is the place, the active agent, and the passive object of worship. All that is fulfilled is fulfilled in Him alone.

This fulfillment did not take place without the abolition, in large measure, of the material. The Temple, from which the Christians were driven out, is destroyed, and cultic worship ceases with its destruction; the priests disappear. Nothing remains of them save the name *Cohen*, meaning priest, adopted by numerous Jewish families who recall belonging to the priestly line. Finally, the animal sacrifices and others also ceased and have not been resumed with the political restoration of Israel.

Of the 613 commandments of the Jewish religion, there remains only the Decalogue, but even in this essential, the ten commandments are reduced to 8, since images are no longer forbidden, but recommended.

What happened was that the abolished Temple became a person: the divine person of Jesus Christ, the one and only priest and the one and only victim. This is the organic teaching of the New Testament: a vital unification, beyond all ritual, where everything is held together in the love of God made man, given up even to death. Thus He is the Temple, the priest and the victim of the unique sacrifice, as he is the *"sole mediator"* (*1 Tim.* 2:5), every other mediation being relative to his.

A TRIPLE ACCOMPLISHMENT IN CHRIST

a) Christ is the Temple.

The Temple was the place of God's presence in the Ark of the Covenant, sign of the indissoluble marriage of God with His people. This presence had been realized at Sinai. The Ark of the Covenant was put within the tent of the divine meeting place. (*Ex.* 40:21-22).

Then,

The cloud covered the tent of meeting,
and the glory of the Lord filled the dwelling
[. . .]
The cloud settled down upon it
and the glory of the Lord
filled it. (Ex. 40:34-35).

Thus the Lord transfers to the Ark, the glory in figure that He had manifested on Sinai, the mountain of God. In the Prologue of John, the Incarnation is presented as a new presence:

"And the Word was made flesh and lived (pitched his tent) *among us." (John* 1:14). He is then the new Tabernacle, the new Tent of the meeting with mankind. Later on we shall see how Mary is involved in this fulfillment of the figures of the Ark and of the Tent.

The Ark, the Tent and the Temple are all the same figure for the presence of God.

"Destroy this temple and in three days I will raise it up," said Jesus. He was speaking of the temple of His body. *(John* 2:21).

This text confirms that the Incarnate Word, and more precisely "His body," is the new temple and that it will replace the old one: a temple of flesh is going to be substituted for a temple of stone.

b) Christ is the Priest.

The temple (being henceforth Jesus in person) is identified at the same time with the unique priest of the New Covenant. The priesthood of Christ remains implicit in the Gospel of *John.* It is made explicit in the Letter to the *Hebrews*, where Jesus is the unique priest. A simple layman with respect to the Jewish priesthood, He belongs "to another line" *(Heb.* 7:6), linked with the mysterious prototype of Melchisedech: *(Heb.* 7:1-25). It is an "eternal" priesthood" characterized by the word *ephapax,* meaning only once (used only five times in the New Testament, three times in the Letter to the *Hebrews* 7:27; 9:12; 10:10).

c) Christ is the Victim of the Unique Sacrifice.

And He is also, at the same time, the unique victim of that unique sacrifice, as set forth by this passage:

By this will (Christ's) we have been sanctified
through the offering of the body of Jesus Christ,
once for all.

Because it is impossible for the blood of bulls
and goats to take sin away [...] Jesus, on com-
ing into the world, said, "Sacrifice and offering
you did not desire, but a body you have pre-
pared for me [...]." Then he said, "I have
come to do your will." (Heb. 10:4-10).

The sacrifice of the eternal priest is the sacrifice of His
own body, of His own life, and for that very reason, it
can only be unique:

Not that he might offer himself again and
again, as the high priest enters year after year
into the sanctuary with blood that is not his own
[...], but he has appeared once for all [...] so
*Christ was offered up once (*ephapax*) to take*
away the sins of many; he will appear a second
time not to take away sin but to bring salvation
to those who eagerly await him. (Heb. 9:25-28).

The uniqueness of the Temple, so strongly emphasized
by the Gospel of *John,* is less clear in the Letter to the
Hebrews than is the uniqueness of Jesus the priest, of the
victim and of the sacrifice. Here the flesh of Christ is no
longer considered as victim, but as the veil of the Temple,
whose rending, at the hour of Christ's death, marked the
end of the Temple and of its sacrifices. It is most fitting
that it is to this place, the Temple, that the body of Christ
is here compared.

MARY'S FOUNDATIONAL ROLE

It is through Mary that the Word "was made flesh"
as we read in *John* 1:14. And it is thus that He became
the temple of God, priest and victim, for it is only in this

passible body and not in His divinity, that He was able to suffer and die for us.

Mary is then at the origin and at the heart of this triple mystery. She was the first to live this triple participation. She is also the prototype and the cultic principle both of the Church and of every Christian.

MARY, THE FIRST CHRISTIAN SANCTUARY

Mary is then a temple, like Christ, like Christians, like the Church. If she is a temple of God through grace, she was the first temple of God made man, who dwelt in her as every child dwells in its mother. She is also the created image of the eternal generation, whereby the Son is in the bosom of the Father. This somatic dwelling of the Son of God is His alone, with a wondrous human and divine quality.

The woman Mary, then, is represented in four stages:

1. First as the Ark of the Covenant in the temple of Heaven.

2. Then as the Woman clothed with the sun.

3. As Mother of the Messiah.

4. Finally, as mother of the disciples, for in the last verse of the chapter, the dragon (Satan) is going to combat the rest of her offspring, those who keep the commandments of God and give witness to Jesus (*Rev.* 12:17).

New theology would like to exclude Mary from Chapter 12 of the Book of *Revelations*. This is really impossible. Formally and expressly the chapter speaks of the Mother of the Messiah. How can one avoid the fact that it is Mary? And this is confirmed by the underlying theology, which is the same in both the Gospels and in *Revelations,* which for many reasons are attributed to the same author.

Christian tradition has rightly perceived and expressed in many ways this data of revelation, Mary's triple participation in the mystery of Christ: temple, priest and victim.

The Fathers of the Church apply to Mary the titles of Temple, Tabernacle, and Ark of the Covenant as early as the fifth century (René Laurentin *Marie, l'Eglise, et le sacerdoce,* Paris, 1952, p. 64-69), and these images of the sanctuary are sometimes linked to those of the priesthood and those of sacrifice.

When Christian temples and basilicas began to be built, people recognized in them a symbol of Mary to whom they were dedicated with a privileged, if not a predominant, frequency that has not diminished in the course of centuries. The Fathers of the Church were very conscious of the connection between temple, priesthood and sacrifice.

The Fathers of the early Church amply demonstrate these connections of Mary with Christ—the Temple, Priest and Victim. For example, Maximus of Turin says:

> In a certain way it is in the sanctuary of her womb that Mary mystically carried the priest, for all that was to save the world came from her womb: God, the Priest and the Victim: the God of the Resurrection, and the Priest of the oblation. All of this we acknowledge in Christ. He is in fact God since he returns to the Father; Pontiff since he offered himself; victim since for us he was put to death. Therefore, I will not call Mary's womb a womb, but a temple (Homily a5, PL 57, 7, 236c).

The Fathers of the Church identify Mary not only with the Temple, but also with the altar and with many objects of the liturgy in the Temple.

Finally, Calvary constituted a terrible spiritual trial for her very faith, as Pope John Paul II indicated in his encyclical *Redemptoris Mater.* The situation on Calvary appeared as the most absolute contradiction of the promise received at the Annunciation:

"Great will be his dignity; the Lord God will give him the throne of David his father. He will rule over the house of Jacob forever" (*Luke* 1:32).

Mary, then, helps us to understand the revolution of

the New Covenant, where ritual worship becomes personal and living, where the temple, priesthood and the ancient sacrifice are centered and united in Jesus Christ. He invites all His members to live and continue this triple mystery until its eschatological fulfillment. Mary is truly the human foundation thereof and its eminent, original, and inspiring model in Jesus Christ.

AND TODAY?

It is particularly important to note that shrines (sanctuaries) are playing a more visible role in the Church. Pope John Paul II, a world traveler and ambassador in the name of the faith, has made many visits to key shrines in the past fifteen years.

We also see the Vatican urging the faithful to visit these sites, stressing the importance of pilgrimage especially to those established and Church recognized shrines. In a world where distance is no longer a hinderance, visits to these established holy places play an important, visible part of our Christian faith.

Part IV

CHAPTER 1

Icons

SPECIFICITY OF THE THEME

Our circuitous route to icons perhaps appears somewhat strange and disconnected. A pilgrimage implies a movement forward and an active participation. A sanctuary is static. It is a firmly established dwelling for God and us. It welcomes us into a three dimensional space. In the icon, we have a colored surface of two dimensions, fashioned in accord with techniques that have been long perfected in oriental tradition.

Let us recall the definition: It is a visible sign, a sacramental, which is a means of grace, intended to lead us through the visible to the invisible, by inspiring contemplative prayer and instilling a sense of mystery.

THE WORDS

The word **icon** comes from the Greek *eikon*, which quite simply means "image." But the sacred meaning given to this Greek word leads us to a long tradition and signifies a sacred image, par excellence.

— Iconography describes and interprets the form of images.

— Iconology refers to an analysis, not only aesthetic, but also religious and philosophical, based on the cultures in which these works were created. It tries to give a total interpretation with the aid of human sciences.

The word appeared in a work by Aby Warburg in 1912. One of the first to use it was Erwin Panofsky in his humanist themes on the art of the Renaissance (Paris, 1967).

THE TURBULENT HISTORY OF THE ICON

It was not without difficulty and uneasiness that the icon took its place in Christian culture. The problem is God's transcendence. Not only is He invisible, but He is beyond all expressibility. Every representation is therefore necessarily inadequate, simplistic, to the point of being a caricature. Furthermore, it can be idolatrous or blasphemous, if one substitutes an image for the ineffable reality. Representation and materialization can offend God. It was to avoid this danger and to impress deeply on the people of God the meaning of transcendence, that Yahweh gave Moses the second commandment of the Decalogue:

"You shall not carve idols for yourselves in the shape of anything in the sky above or on the earth below or in the waters beneath the earth" (*Deut.* 5:8).

Deuteronomy states the reasons for this prescription, often renewed in the Bible:

You saw no form at all on the day the Lord spoke to you at Horeb from the midst of the fire. Be strictly on your guard, therefore, not to degrade yourselves by fashioning an idol to represent any figure, whether it be in the form of a man or of a woman, of any animal on the earth or of any bird that flies in the sky, of anything that crawls on the ground or of any fish in the waters under the earth. And when you look up into the heavens and behold the sun or the moon or any star among the heavenly hosts,

*do not be led astray into adoring them and serv-
ing them. These the Lord, your God, has let fall
to the lot of all other nations under the heavens;
but you he has taken and led out of that iron
foundry, Egypt, that you might be his very own
people (Deut. 4:215-20).*

God inculcates the meaning of His transcendance by
forbidding images. He communicates less through sight
than through hearing: *"Hear, O Israel"* is the key word
and one of the refrains of the Bible (*Deut. 4:1*).

Islam, like Judaism, has observed this law. All the same,
there are exceptions in the Old Testament: two cherubim
on the Ark of the Covenant.

It was this fundamental biblical law that seemed to
make it a duty to support iconoclasm, which destroyed
images violently. The word comes from the Greek *klaō*,
meaning to break.

The crisis broke out during the Isaurian dynasty. The
causes have been explained in various ways, notably, fear
of Islam, iconoclastic by reason of the precepts in the
Koran.

Yazid II (724), caliph at Damascus, ruled against every
image of a living being "because the image is mute, does
not breathe, is not of the same substance as the person
represented." These arguments were taken up by Emperor
Leo III, who ordered the destruction of images, beginning
in 724. His son, Constantine V, assembled the Council of
Hieria (August 28, 753), which banned images as idolatry.
The sole image of Christ is the Eucharist, proclaimed the
Council. There followed a violent persecution, which had
its martyrs.

After the death of Leo IV, his wife, Irene, in accord
with the Pope, convoked the Seventh Ecumenical Council
of Nicaea (787), which defined the meaning of the cult
of images in a correct line that steered between iconoclasm and idolatry:

The honor given to an image passes to its prototype [which it represents]. Whoever venerates the image, venerates in it the hypostasis [the underlying reality] of that which is painted. The Council rightly defines the difference between adoration due to God alone, and veneration due to icons. Those who contemplate them are led to recall the prototypes...In kissing them, they show them a respectful veneration which is not a true adoration, which according to our faith, is fitting for God alone (Denzinger Schönmetzer 601).

On September 14, 1987, for the twelfth centenary of the Second Council of Nicaea, the Patriarch Dimitrios I of Constantinople, published an "Encyclical on the Theology of the Icon," translated in *Documentation Catholique,* March 20, 1988, no. 1958, p. 323-328.

The crisis, however, did return. There was a second period of iconoclasm between 813 and 843. After the death of Emperor Theophilus, the Empress Theodora replaced the Patriarch with Methodius, who with great pomp celebrated the definitive victory over "craven images," commemorated by the Feast of Orthodoxy, celebrated to this day on the first Sunday of Lent.

The Orient knew how to "baptize" the image: to purify and spiritualize it. It has thus become the master of Christian iconography. On the contrary, Latin iconography is, in large measure, a history of oscillations and aberrations. Western religious painting, which is more free, has often seen the exaltation of art as art, an aestheticism without reference to the sacred, an exaltation of the human body, even to the point of eroticism and perversions of eros. Botticelli used the same model (his mistress it seems) for both Venus and the Virgin Mary. Certain modern representations paint Christ from a homosexual standpoint.

It is strange that the Church, so vigilant and so critical in matters of doctrine, has been so lax in matters of art and images, and has not known how to establish norms, or has she had sufficient discernment to promote authentic icons and condemn or set aside those that are foreign to the faith. In this area, heresies are legion, and have never been condemned or censured. Writings are censured. Apparitions are censured, often without examination. The religious art in our churches is very seldom censured. It is one of the strengths of the Eastern Church that it has maintained a vibrant liturgical tradition, inspired by the icon. This liturgy evolves from the interior, not from the efforts of technocrats. It contributes to the promotion and the understanding of icons much better than the Western Church. In that Church, icons have become an important sacramental, not without a tendency to make of them a quasi-sacrament: the location of a "hypostatic" presence. This ambiguous word often turns up in Oriental theology to signify the underlying (hypostatic) reality of the model: God, Christ, or the Blessed Virgin. The Eastern Church expresses the presence of God in the icon in terms analogous to the Eucharistic presence.

Of course all is not perfect in eastern iconography. By turns fought against or enthusiastically cultivated, despised or overpraised, it has had its successes and its declines.

In the sad state of our Western iconography, the sense of the faithful has seen in the icon a norm and a remedy. In large measure, people see Eastern icons as a substitute for our failing iconography. In an encyclical, the Patriarch Dimitrios recommended the private use of icons.

> "Icons may never be treated as commercial articles or as objects to be engraved on paper or other material of little value, using the present methods of industrial reproduction in order to reap profits. Still less is their circulation to

be augmented in some illicit manner in today's secularized society. We consider these usages to be sacrilegious and impious, as a very serious affront and an insult to the sacred character of the icon, this great spiritual acquisition of the Holy Orthodox Church" (nos. 31 and 32 of the encyclical).

Since the overstepping of the precept in the Decalogue is based on the Incarnation, the ecumenical council of 787 forbade the representation of the Father, a pure spirit and source of divinity. This also holds true for the Holy Spirit. The only form that is not questionable is the symbolic dove at the baptism of Christ, which Western painters place between the Father and the Son, between the beard of the first and the fine head of hair of the second.

MATERIAL DEFINITION

The icon, in the strict sense of the word (that is to say, a Christian image in the Oriental tradition), is a painting on wood, that has been prepared with a sizing, a white ground (Greek, *leukas,* meaning white), made up of a paste and a plaster powder. The colors, mixed with egg, are set down in layers, more and more, which preserve an effect of transparence. In this way, "all the orders, vegetable and animal, have a part in this sacramentalization of beauty," as Olivier Clement summed up so well.

THEOLOGICAL DEFINITION

The icon is a sacred representation of the invisible, totally relative to God and to the heavenly universe of which God is the measure. It is inserted within God's orbit and is intended to be its manifestation and brilliance.

It can be understood in the Greek platonic perspective, where the world here below is only the shadow of the transcendant. For Plato, it was the world of ideas of which we see only the vague semblance in the cavern of this world. For the Greek Fathers, ideas are the thought of

God, models and projected schemes for his creation. Using this spiritual prototype, the icon is the material representation.

HYPOSTATIC STRUCTURE OF THE ICON

As distinguished from profane painting, which is sensual and realistic, in forms as diverse as classic painting and impressionist painting, the icon paradoxically tries to show the invisible in a way that is unavoidably inadequate. Over the course of centuries, it has succeeded, in unequal measure, to do this through a certain number of remarkable norms and procedures, governed by the ascetical and mystical inspiration of Orthodoxy.

The factors that make up the icon are:

— Christ and the saints are represented frontally. The icon is an encounter.

— The body, disproportionately elongated, becomes totally a visage, and the visage becomes totally a look. Then too the icon is transparence. It is not an object in a show window that one looks at. It is something that looks at us. This trait is essential.

— The composition is relativized: animals, plants and matter are stylized, spiritualized, immaterialized. Architectural elements, always in the background, are less realist than surrealist, and heighten the sacred atmosphere.

— The icon knows nothing of perspective or anything that would give the illusion of relief, such as the illusionism of certain super-realist painters who can give the impression that a knife is really in the picture, that some object is about to detach itself, or that a fruit offers itself to your hand. Even more, in the icon perspective is reversed. The lines of perspective do not give the illusion of relief, but on the contrary, invite the one who is looking at the icon to enter into it...and past the icon towards the beyond.

— Finally, the icon, in a manner all its own, tries to capture light. It is not through the technique of a play between shadow and light, of which classical painting produces some striking contrasts. In the icon, light does not come from any one source. It is the very foundation of the icon, which the painters call light. Everything is lit up from the interior. The body and garments are illuminated with fine hachures of gold.

Nevertheless, the icon is realistic. The symbols of the earliest Christian art, fish or lamb, are replaced by the direct representation of what they prefigured: the human visage of God made man, or the image of man divinized. This visage is transfigured. Unobtrusively, silently, it radiates the glory of God.

Unlike a statue, an icon does not have relief, it ventures all on color, the most vibrant matter in the visible universe. The two dimensions of the icon abstract from relief. They flatten it and bypass it in transparence.

THE COLORS

Each of the colors has a meaning as detailed by Egon Sendler in *"The Icon, Image of the Invisible,"* a study of technique (Paris, DDB, 1981).

— Blue is the color of transcendance. It is the least tangible and the most spiritual of all the colors. It produces an impression of profundity and calm. It gives one the feeling of an unreal world, one without weight.

— Red is the most active color. It moves towards the spectator. It is assertive. It is incandescence.

— Royal and priestly purple, an imported product, evokes richness. The best icons exalt the richness of humility as we see in the icon of Vladimir: a humble mother with her child on a ground of gold.

A curious thing: the one who explains these symbols seems to know nothing of yellow. He knows only gold, which concentrates the brilliance of light.

In short, the icon is intended to be a simple, modest, unembellished sign, without any searching after effect or virtuosity. It does not wish to call attention to itself, as a pictorial production.

CHAPTER 2

Theology of the Icon

It intends to be and is, in great measure, not a screen that is interposed, but an opening upon the beyond, on the invisible world that is our homeland.

The icon does not end in the picture, but in the reality that it represents: in God Himself, and whom the believer reaches through the icon. It is completely directed towards this reality. It directs us toward the same.

The icon is treated as a sacred object, venerated and kept in the shrine, where it adorns the iconostasis. In homes a corner shrine is often made for it, placed so as to greet visitors and those who dwell there.

A CERTAIN PRESENCE

Eastern theology insists on the presence of hypostasis (that of the person represented), which it assures the faithful.

Then would the icon ever be considered a sacrament? No! A sacrament is a sign instituted by Jesus Christ which infallibly brings about salvific acts.

ICON AND INCARNATION

The icon is based on the Incarnation of Jesus-Christ, but it was not instituted by Him. And it does not automatically procure grace, but only according to the piety

74

of the one who prays before the icon.

Nevertheless, the great veneration accorded to icons would tend to grant them something more.

John Damascene considers the icon "as filled with energy and grace."

> "This expression, not free of ambiguity and the danger of fetishism, states, in a metaphoric way, that the body of Christ communicates its holiness to other material objects. Thus the icon becomes an entitative participation in the body of Christ: it would be close to the sacraments.
>
> "In fact, certain fanatics considered them to be superior to the sacraments, even going so far as to add fragments of icons to the holy eucharistic species! Evidently, this practice was condemned by the Orthodox Church" (E. Sendler, p. 47).

To improperly give the supernatural a physical, radioactive form in order to see in it some kind of energy or magic would falsify its nature. This is a materialistic illusion analogous to that of the brothers Bogdanov (*God And Science*, Grasset, 1991), who seem to confound energizing waves with the spiritual (but a wave is quantifiable, and the spiritual is not).

But God does not impart to the icon a power that would objectively sanctify it simply because of what it is. In that case, even an icon that has deteriorated would embody a presence. Following St. Germain, St. Theodore concedes that one may burn an icon that is no longer usable, like wood that is now useless (pg. 90, 334).

The presence is not that of an "energy" but of "the hypostasis," say the Fathers; that is to say, of the personal reality of God or of Christ, from the fact that the icon represents the characteristic traits of the prototype.

In this regard, Saint Theodore presents a suggestive comparison, drawn from the correspondence between a seal and its imprint:

Let us take, for example, a ring on which is engraved an image of the emperor. If it be pressed upon wax, pitch or clay, the seal will remain unchangeably the same in each of these materials, however different they may be. The seal would not remain the same in these materials if it in some way partook of their nature. But it is in fact separate from them and it remains in the ring. Similarly, the semblance of Christ, when imprinted in any kind of material into which it is imprinted, for it remains in the hypostasis of Christ to which it properly belongs (*Letter to Plato*, pgs. 99, 504-505).

ICON AND SACRAMENTS

He concludes that the icon therefore does not belong to the order of sacraments. The matter of the sacraments is an instrument for the grace of God. The water of baptism sanctifies through the power of the Holy Spirit. The icon does not have us partake of Christ substantially, as does the Eucharistic bread, which is the body of Christ. It makes us participate in the hypostasis of Christ by way of relation, and this participation is of the intentional order, with respect to the person represented.

In short, the icon is relationship. It is only an internationa relation to that other world, invisible to us, which it represents. It is this reality of the beyond, a reality essentially personal, that the Greeks speak of as "hypostasis," and they qualify as hypostatic the relation of the icon with God, in the same sense as the humanity of Christ subsists in His person.

Here hypostasis seems to mean the underlying reality which the icon represents and renders present, which is the person of Christ.

ICON AND EUCHARIST

If the icon is totally relative to what it represents and renders present, may it be compared to the Eucharist, of which one can say the same thing?

There is an analogy, for the visible species of bread and wine sybolically represent and render truly present the body of Christ, which is in Heaven. In both cases (icon and Eucharist), the sign refers completely to the reality. The analogy goes too far, for Christ is not in the host as in a box. The host loses all of its own reality (by transubstantiation, according to Aristotelian philosophy) and no longer subsists except in appearance. And thus this body is really present wherever the host is, but this does not involve a localization upon every single altar, as Thomas Aquinas makes clear. The body is really, corporally present, but in a spiritual mode. It is therefore we who are rendered present to the one body of Christ, and not He who would have to be multiplied to descend physically into a multitude of hosts.

Christ is not present to the same degree in the icon, which keeps its entire physical substance: the wood remains wood, and the painting remains a painting; while the host is no longer bread, although it keeps all the appearances thereof.

The point common to both the Eucharist and the icon is that they are signs and mediate a presence but in different ways for:

— without changing its appearance, Christ assumes the host in the Eucharist, where we do not see His face,

— but it is His features that the icon presents to us pictorially.

THE ICON IN THE THEOLOGY OF RELATIONSHIP

Here we are at the heart of theology, which is essentially the understanding of relation in all the diversity of its forms. Theology gets us to know not so much God in Himself (for He is ineffable), as much as our relationship to God. And it is through our relation with Him that we know Him.

This has far-reaching consequences, for God, being transcendant, this relationship creates no changes. The foundation and the change implied by the relation is therefore entirely from the side of the creature. It is only the creature that is affected, and it is in the creature that the reality of the true relation resides.

This transcendental relationship to God is differentiated according to each mystery, and defined precisely by the specificity of each relation.

The icon brings about a different kind of relation: an intentional one. It represents Christ (or Mary) and makes Him morally present by means of an unpretentious picture of His human features. This presence is brought about when Christians, through this sign, contemplate the love that results. Grace activates the union that comes about through this contemplation.

PARTICIPATION

From the point of view of eastern theology, the presence and the communion that come through the icon can be described as participation in the divine.

According to St. John Damascene (*Discourse against those who reject images,* around 730), the image is a participation in the prototype it represents. Through it, this participation is not merely symbolic or poetic, but has an ontological aspect.

But John Damascene was aware that this created participation is never adequate. There is always a disparity between the prototype and the created participation: the image is similar to, but always differs, in some way, from that which it represents (pg. 94, 1240). The degree of likeness depends on the degree of participation in the prototype, just as a faithful image differs according to whether it is photographic, pictorial, cinematographic, or other. The perfection of the image, he explains, exists only in the Holy Trinity.

THE SPIRITUAL MEANING OF THE ICON

The icon displays its homogeneous, vital value in three stages, where everything comes from God and through faith returns to Him.

First, the painter of an icon is traditionally a person of prayer. It is by fasting and in solitude that the inspiration develops. Thus the icon comes from God in its very origin and in its composition.

Second, the icon, thus produced under the influence of a transcendant model, brings about a resemblance to, and a participation in the divine model.

Third, in contemplating the icon, praying before it, and through it, coming into touch with what it represents, the faithful adapt themselves to this resemblance. This intentional identification in prayer is taken up and raised by grace.

Such is the spirituality of the icon: everything is reference to God, forgetfulness of self, grace and participation at all levels.

Although there is a market for icons and there are icon museums, the icon is not, in itself, an aesthetic object that one acquires, but a gratuitous encounter and a visible channel for prayer. It is a window opening up to the invisible.

THE BLESSED VIRGIN IN ICONOGRAPHY

In iconography, as elsewhere, the Blessed Virgin holds a prominent position. It is she who is most frequently represented, all the more insofar as she is integrally part of the depictions of Christ, who was inseparable from His Mother, at least during His infancy.

The iconography of the Blessed Virgin developed from the interior, through the pure vision of faith, into a certain number of types.

HISTORICAL OVERVIEW

The first representations of the Blessed Virgin appear sporadically in the catacombs. Dating from the third century, in the cemetery of Priscilla, there is a drawing of a mother, evidently seated, clasping a nude infant in her arms. A star is shown above them. As early as the fourth century, we find the type of the *orante*, her two arms raised. Jesus stands out transparently on her breast. This is the prototype called *Blachernitissa*.

During the era of the basilicas, beginning with the conversion of Constantine, we have a royal iconography. The Blessed Virgin, in majesty, is seated on a throne and she herself serves as a throne for the Infant Jesus. She receives the homage and the gifts of the Magi. Then comes the type of the *Hodigitria* (the guide, the leader), standing between Michael and Gabriel, who bow, full of reverence, and who pay her homage with a terrestrial globe surmounted by a cross, sign of the royalty of Jesus and of her own.

The *Eleusa,* is the Virgin of Tenderness. Here the Infant puts His arm around her neck, His cheek against that of His Mother. The most beautiful example of this type is the Vladimir icon.

The illustration of the life of Mary is very rich—from the apocryphal accounts of her infancy, beginning with the Protogospel of James from the middle of the second century, to the apocryphal accounts of her death, which are more difficult to date. Bagatti traces them back to the second century. Others move them up to the fourth and fifth centuries, passing over the Gospel episodes that became mysteries of the Rosary: the Annunciation, the Visitation, the Nativity, the Presentation, the Finding in the Temple, not forgetting Calvary.

In the West, our iconography, for a long time dependent on the Orient, began to fly with its own wings, beginning with the Carolingian era. It is restrained, for the West remained marked by the repercussions of iconoclasm, without going so far as to destroy the images. But Romanesque churches exhibit a great sobriety in this respect.

In the Gothic cathedrals of the thirteenth century there is a full range of images embracing the entire history of salvation from the creation to the fall, to the prophets, to the mysteries of Christ and to the saints, with an extraordinary abundance. It was iconography different from that of the East, but profoundly inspired by meditation on the Gospel. But in departing from that, the West turned toward naturalism: from the Renaissance to Rubens, and to the decorative and ornamental riotousness of the Baroque.

Western iconography of the Blessed Virgin had begun in the twelfth century with Romanesque Virgins (sculpted in the style of the pictures in manuscripts), the calm throne, a frontal image like that of the Oriental icons. These representations were realistic, with the Virgin sometimes having the appearance of a rough peasant, but hieratic and fixed in a kind of sacred abstraction. The gaze of the Blessed Virgin and of the Infant upon the viewer was full of meaning. The inspiration was the same as that for the icons.

In the thirteenth century the Virgin became affable and smiling. They presented to us her smile as much as they did her son. The Child Jesus seemed to lose His central position and moved over to the side. In place of a sober and hieratic garment, artists substituted feminine finery with complicated folds.

Quite often, popular piety begins to dress statues, then covers over the white silk robe with jewels. The statue disappears beneath the garments and the garments beneath the jewels. Painting and sculpture fall into mannerisms as well.

In the fifteenth century, the Virgin at Calvary, standing at the foot of the cross (the *Stabat*), collapses in a swoon. Sermons speak of her tears, her sighs and her weaknesses. Too often they forget to speak of her courage, the trial of her faith, and her cooperation in the work of salvation.

It is easy to understand why Protestantism, anxious to return to the essential (God alone, Christ alone) would point to the first commandment of the Decalogue in reaction against a decadent iconography. This is one aspect of the Protestant crisis. The iconography of the Counter Reformation often reacted in an opposite way, by adopting mannerism and naturalism: which was not the point at isssue.

Our era, powerless to express the sacred, often takes refuge in the abstract. Modern man no longer knows how and no longer wishes to represent to himself what is beyond: Heaven, Hell and Purgatory, which fascinated previous generations. Is it modesty, powerlessness, or a lack of faith? Our iconography is, as it were, exhausted.

In 1964, trying to exercise this powerlessness of religious art, I invited artists, on the occasion of the centenary of the statue of Lourdes, to illustrate the description that Bernadette had made of the Virgin of the Grotto. The entries showed, in large measure, that most of today's artists are not at all ready to illustrate this subject. Many used this as an excuse.

In the exhibition, which was presented at Paris and then at Lourdes, there were at least some worthwhile responses. Two of them in particular.

— In figurative art, Dubos sculpted on old wood of Mary and Bernadette, both small and young (according to the seer's description), humble and transparent.

— Hartung, one of the great painters of the century, illustrated the abstract expression with which Bernadette designated the apparition at Lourdes. It was a ray of light emerging from the night, the Immaculate One emerging from this world of sin.

WHY IS MARY IMPORTANT IN ICONOGRAPHY?

1. She is, like Christ, a visible person, unlike the angels or the saints whose bodies have not been raised up. This particular reason has been able to influence iconography.

2. "She is most beautiful," Christian tradition constantly states, certain that spiritual beauty is reflected in bodily beauty. In some ways this is always true, for the marks of spiritual beauty are not the aesthetic or erotic canons that prevail at the election of beauty queens.

3. She is a mother, and maternity, in a high degree, is

something tangible and picturable. She brings together the beauty proper to a woman with the touching beauty of the child full of promise. The intimacy of their relationship speaks to the human heart.

More profoundly, maternity is the very origin of all life and of all human awakening. It is also the masterpiece of creation, the summit of the gift of love, for the Creator has placed within the heart of women a capacity for the gift of self which does not exist in the heart of men, so necessary to form and raise a child. The mother is then a privileged symbol of love. Her body is like her psychological make-up, fashioned and actuated to give the most essential gift to every human life.

Within this masterpiece of nature created by God, Mary, Mother of God and of mankind, is, in this respect, the supernatural and divine culmination, ineffable and breathtaking. On this score also, she has something with which to inspire painters.

She is also an image of suffering, through her presence on Calvary: standing at the foot of the cross, according to *John* 19:25-27, or as the Pietá receiving the dead body of her Son upon her knees. According to a survey made in Italy, this is the most popular image of the Virgin Mary. It has inspired the most beautiful masterpieces of painting, notably the *Pietá* of Avignon. To this, one can add all the icons of the crucifixion. Suffering is one of the sources of inspiration for painting, an entire domain of dramatic and tragic beauty.

Finally, Mary is an image of glory, also a source of inspiration. She is now the zenith of glory in God. The painting of her Assumption and her Coronation has inspired numerous masterpieces, evoking her presence and her power. Gospel scenes (the Annunciation and the Visitation, first of all), also have a great value and aesthetic potential.

The iconography of the Blessed Virgin (like iconography in general) is a gamble, for how can one visibly represent the invisible? And the Blessed Virgin is invisible on two counts.

1. Historically, we must repeat St. Augustine: "For we have not known the face of the Blessed Virgin." And St. Luke has only given us her psychological portrait in *Luke* 1:2.

2. And her divine glory escapes us today. The seers, to whom she shows herself are overwhelmed by her ineffable beauty. For them the ineffable is something only they experience.

Iconography often inclines toward naturalism and sometimes hastens down that road. It is fitting that it remain concrete, close to nature, for Jesus is true man at the same time as true God. There is no question then of making Him a superman, of absorbing His humanity in a fantastic or etherialized representation of His divinity. Like His Mother (who expresses the same attitudes in the Infancy Narratives, *Luke* 1:38 and 48) his condition is that of a servant and of a poor man. Iconography must not forget this. But it must not forget, even more, that the model surpasses its powers. The icon is an art of humility.

Nevertheless, this modesty is not enough. It is necessary that beyond its realism it evoke in some manner the divine transfiguration of countenances and all reality.

PART V

CHAPTER 1

Apparitions

Apparitions are among the most poorly studied of phenomena. There is not an exhaustive historic survey, or even one that is at least somewhat serious; there is no evaluation of the whole problem worthy of the name. I am planning a dictionary to remedy this lack with two other specialists, Joachim Bouflet and Sylvie Barnay.

Because of this crass ignorance, apparitions remain subject to uncontrolled crazes and to repressions, or to marginalizations that are often poorly informed. In this matter, what is most lacking is discernment.

But first of all, what is an apparition? It is the visible and unexpected manifestation of someone or something, the sight of which in such and such a place, or at such and such a moment, is unusual or inexplicable in the normal course of events.

In the religious domain, it can be of a being invisible by nature: an angel, a separated soul, or God Himself; or of a visible person who does not belong to our space-time, as is the case with the Virgin Mary. Of herself, she is visible insofar as she is glorified in her body. On the other hand, she belongs not to the successive duration of our time, but to the eternal duration of God.

HISTORICAL OVERVIEW

In the Bible, apparitions are frequent (from Abraham and Moses to the prophets), and in the New Testament, where angels appear as in the Infancy Narratives (*Matt.* 1:20-24; 2:13, 19; *Luke* 1:11-38; 2:9-15) then in the agony in the garden (*Luke* 22:43) and at the Resurrection of Christ (*Matt.* 28:2, 5; *Luke* 24:33; *John* 20:12). There is also the apparition of Moses and Elias at the Transfiguration (*Mark* 9:4 and its parallels), and above all, those of the risen Christ Himself as given in all four Gospels. In the *Acts of the Apostles* apparitions are numerous:
— the tongues of fire at Pentecost (2, 3)
— Stephen's vision (7, 56)
— Saul's vision (9, 5)
— those of Ananias (9, 10), Cornelius (10, 3-6) and of Peter at Joppa (10)
— and in prison (12, 7-11) etc.

Apparitions and locutions have been constant throught the ages. They are, therefore, a normal dimension of Christian life, although they are relatively exceptional.

They have the same function as icons: to render the invisible, visible. Icons do this through human manufacture; apparitions, as a gift of God, or else as a play of human subjectivity, hence the need for discernment.

As for the Protestants, they insist with such force on the spiritual and its lack of ornamentation, that they have cultivated a faith deprived of images, following the precept of the Decalogue. This abstraction gives rise among them to many reactions in the form of pietistic revivals with a breaking out of charism, and bodily actions such as prophesy or other charisms, notably healings.

The need for images is fundamental, for we are incapable of thinking without images, though they may be reduced to a very minimum. Prayer disappears into distraction if it does not have the support of some kind of image, however tenuous it may be. St. Ignatius asks that prayer begin very concretely with the "composition of

place": the Infant Jesus in the crib, the Lord healing, in
agony, or crucified. In prayer there is a functional and
perceptible continuity between "compositions" of the
imagination, —the inspirations that vivify them, —the
visions "of the heart," as Jelena of Medjugorje says so
appropriately, —and the exterior and perceptible apparitions of certain seers such as those testified to in Medjugorje among others.

There is not a functional difference between these four
degrees, nor such a thing as a difference in value. If
knowledge is more perceptible in an apparition than in
a vision, and in a vision more than in a composition of
place, the more perceptible is not necessarily the better.
The spiritual value and the quality of love ascend by
another mystical ladder. That is why Jesus declares:
   Blessed are those who have not seen and have believed,
(*John* 20:29).
   That being said, the nature of apparitions (authentic
ones) is that they are a gratuitous gift of Heaven. This
does not mean that they have an absolute and infallible
value, for this communication, filtered through the capacity of the seer, always involves that person's cooperation.
"Whatever is received is received according to the capacity
of the receiver," as the scholastic adage rightly says. Apparitions generally speak the language of the country where
they occur, and are marked with the character of the cultural and visual universe of that locale. Each visionary
keeps his or her own style when they transmit the words
of Christ or of the Blessed Virgin, even when they think
they are transcribing them literally. Here, there are two
factors at play that are more or less complementary and
difficult to distinguish:
— God's adaption to the visionary
— the active participation of the latter in the interpretation, memorization, and transcription.

NATURE OF APPARITIONS

In addition to the definition stated above, there are the following questions and characteristics.

What is the nature of these communications of the supernatural rendered visible? God has different ways of communicating with man on the perceptible level. They include exterior apparitions or interior visions, as we have already indicated, a concrete manifestation of a person or of a symbol, notably fire.

Visions are easily reduced to a product of the imagination, but the impression of those who authentically have this experience is that they enter into contact, not with a dream, but with a world more real than the one to which they afterwards return. They no longer fear death, but hope to die so that they might once again see what alone has value for them. This dimension of an authentic clairvoyance has not been taken into consideration sufficiently.

The study of this mode of communication remains in its infancy. Most frequently it is easily interpreted in the way an idealist philosophy or psychoanalysis would suggest: that it is pure subjectivity. On the other hand, those who are enthusiasts about apparitions liken them to meeting a person of this world; which seems to be supported by the expression of certain seers like Catherine Labouré or Bernadette Soubirous:

"I see her the way I see you."

But scientific study, recently begun with the encephalogram and other instruments, shows that the visions experienced as the most objective do not pass through the ordinary channels. There is no image of the Blessed Virgin on the retina of the seers. And during the apparition, the stimuli of the ordinary world move along the optic or auditory nerve of the visionary in ecstasy as the study of the senses in activity has demonstrated. Those who reduce apparitions to subjectivity conclude that this confirms that every vision or apparition is a hallucination. But in other respects, there are numerous indications of objectivity, notably the synchronizations of the seers who are having the same apparition. Synchronizations such as these can come only from the influence of the apparition. I analyzed ten of these in the book *Is the Virgin Appearing at Medjugorje?*

1. The seers kneel down in a way perfectly synchronized (without any sign or signal) when the Blessed Virgin appears.

2. When their voices recite the "Our Father" or the "Hail Mary," they die out simultaneously and from then on they emit no sound, even when they speak with the apparition.

3. The voices reappear in a surprisingly simultaneous way to pray with Our Lady.

4. They do not pronounce the first two words of the "Our Father," which the Blessed Virgin begins. They link up with "who art in heaven," which surprised many of the early witnesses.

5. The voices fade away again simultaneously at the end of this prayer recited with Our Lady, and their conversations, quite lively, once again become silent.

6. At the end of the apparition, eyes and heads are raised together, because, say the seers, "She disappears by going up."

7. At the moment when their eyes and heads reach the highest point, one or several seers (simultaneously) say *ode*, that is, "She is gone."

8. At the beginning of the ecstasy, the eyeballs stop their ordinary movement in observation. Normally our eye moves in order to observe and perception takes place at a level more immediate, purely intuitive. With the seers this stopping of the eyeball's movement occurs synchronically within about a fifth of a second, as established by a simultaneous oculogram performed on Ivan and Marija on 28 December 1984.

9. From the beginning of the ecstasy, the brain's beta rhythm (rhythm of reflexion and activity: 18 cycles per second) gradually disappears, and the alpha rhythm

(much slower: ten cycles per second) spreads throughout the whole brain as some encephalograms at Medjugorje demonstrate. But there are many variations depending on the seers, and the activity in which they are engaged during the course of the apparition with the one who appears to them.

10. The end of the apparition likewise is revealed by the markings on the encephalogram. The beta rhythm reappears in various degrees, depending on the seer. This ensemble of ten synchronizations observed with several of the seers (from two to five, depending on circumstances) defies any explanation by way of subjectivity or (as some have tried to do without any psychiatric basis) by collective hallucination.

In another connection, the electro-encephalograms show that the seer in ecstasy is not asleep, does not dream, and is not in a state of epilepsy. The ensemble of tests excludes any pathological hallucination, according to the conclusions of Professor Joyeux in *Medical and Scientific Studies at Medjugorje* (Paris, OEIL, 1985, p. 97). Other studies have been carried out with all sorts of tests by Italian doctors from ARPA, at Medjugorje, and elsewhere, on other seers. These are only the first experimental stages in a scientific study of this complex phenomenon.

STATUS OF APPARITIONS

Apparitions have a very humble place in the Church, in keeping with the words of Christ: *Blessed are those who have not seen and have believed* (*John* 20:29).

To this is added the fear of illusion and illuminism, and the offense which the seers' direct line with Heaven might give to the Church's Magisterium. This has been the occasion for and the motive behind many repressions. The cult of radical and suspicious criticism, the stress on subjectivity made by idealism, the dominant philosophy of our day and the psychoanalysis born thereof, have contributed to devaluing apparitions in the public opinion, be it secular, Catholic, or clerical.

Apparitions and visions have as their function the re-awakening of faith (often asleep, smothered), and the re-awakening of "hope above all," as says Thomas Aquinas.

THE SURPRISING IMPORTANCE OF APPARITIONS

Why do apparitions, so greatly devalued for so many good reasons, still hold such a place in the life of the Church, as in the Bible, down through the ages and up to our own day? After St. Peter's in Rome, the greatest shrines in the world are shrines where apparitions took place. Let us consider Guadalupe in Mexico, Aparecida in Brazil, Lourdes in France, Fatima in Portugal, etc.

This appears to be both a human reaction and a compensatory aid against the theological and administrative abstraction that is often rampant in the Church. We have previously noted the reactions to radical suffocation in the churches springing from the Reformation. The same problem exists in the Catholic Church, which to a large extent has been aligned, it must be said, with Protestantism in reducing the nutrients of popular religion during the decades since Vatican Council II.

This situation explains the current malaise affecting apparitions: enthusiasm on the part of some, repression on the part of others. Between these two extreme attitudes, a prudent middle ground is needed. It has been realized by certain bishops in the better cases, which are none too frequent.

THE MULTIPLICATION OF APPARITIONS

Why do apparitions seem to keep on multiplying today? The phenomenon is more complex than it appears.

There is first of all a juridical and administrative reason. Until 14 October 1966, canon 1399, §5 of the old Code of Canon Law "forbade book and brochures that recount new apparitions, revelations, visions, prophecies or miracles and set forth new devotions, even those under the pretext that they are private." Canon 2318 excommunicated offenders.

Paul VI abolished these canons on 14 October 1966. These articles, therefore, have not been inserted into the new Code of Canon Law. Apparitions are no longer under a bushel basket.

Under these conditions, people have again begun to publish and speak about them. The end of that heavy silence has facilitated the blossoming of apparitions. The charism, censured exteriorly and thus through obedience repressed interiorly, has been awakened.

This is not an isolated case. The charism of speaking in tongues, which seemed to have disappeared, has been multiplied since its new burgeoning in the charismatic renewal and has made many Christians eager to obtain it. Some have prayed for this, have prepared for it, have exercised it, so that at the beginning of the seventies this charism spread wide among thousands, tens of thousands. Evidently, apparitions have been much less extensive.

In the new conditions created by the abolition of Canon 1399, we can ask: Are there more apparitions? Or is it only that they are talked about more?

There is, in fact, an increase on both levels. This is due solely neither to the liberating of what had been forbidden, nor to the new religious elan which has fostered this charism.

At a time when faith is being smothered, or finds itself suffocated in many ways, Heaven has been able to come and help Christians revive their faith. It is a fact that conversions are multiplied at Medjugorje and in numerous places of apparitions.

If one believes certain apocalyptic and eschatological messages, this multiplication may be due to the fact that our age is going through a transition and a serious crisis, the end of an era, if not the end of time itself. The future will judge. At a time in civilization when the image of man is ordinarily sensual, erotic, garish, and marked by worldly display, Heaven may wish to intervene.

HOW TO DISCERN THE AUTHENTICITY OF APPARITIONS

Discernment is a complex thing. It is most often approached with an over-simplification that is truly disconcerting, even on the highest intellectual levels, including the hierarchy. Authenticity and inauthenticity are not susceptible to being cut apart with a knife. Every apparition is an ambiguous phenomenon. The supernatural becoming perceptible is ambiguous from the fact that it is addressed to a human sensibility. It is so complex due to the necessary interaction between a divine motion and a human receptivity. This complex mixture does not offer absolute simplicity and transparency.

I have seen both adversaries and devotees of apparitions scandalized, and condemning apparitions for the simple reason that a seer contact with God can be mistaken in case of a prediction. This has happened throughout the history of Christian hagiography. One day a good priest, who had been receptive to some apparently serious apparitions, sent me a fax with an urgent appeal, saying in substance: the seer seemed to have foreseen her death at Easter. She did not die. Should I put an end to our prayer meetings, after having denounced the error which discredits these apparitions?

This reaction does honor to the earnestness and the conscientiousness of this priest; but I, in conscience and understanding the nature of the case, considered it my duty to tell him, in substance:

> "The seer has been mistaken in this circumspect prediction (and one that was otherwise quite secret) that she made known to you. As many seers, she could confound her own interior impulses with God's motions. It will be necessary to speak to her one day about this and have a discernment made, with the benefits of humility and prudence that will result for her therefrom. But since her prediction was in no way

a public one, this private affair should be settled privately. There is no reason to discontinue fruitful prayer, which until now has been a pure source of grace and of spiritual or physical healings without disorder of any kind."

I give this example to show concretely the complexity involved in discernment.

A. Do these apparitions conform to faith and morals? Any deviation in these areas would constitute a principal negative sign.

B. Are the seers sincere, truthful or deceitful, well-balanced, objective, disinterested, coherent? Is their life, their attitude, a good testimony?

C. Are they normal? Are their ecstasies of a pathological nature?

D. Are there signs from Heaven, miracles or extraordinary occurrences (the principal ones and those most often cited in the Gospels being cures?)

E. Finally and above all, are there spiritual fruits? According to the criteria of Christ Himself: *"A good tree cannot bear bad fruit, a bad tree cannot bear good fruit."* This principle of the Gospel is contested today. It is fashionable to say, as does Bishop Zanic at Medjugorje, that "an apparition may be true or false, a relic true or false, the graces are the same." It seems to me that this slogan does not correspond with spiritual experience. Of course, human errors can be the occasion of grace. God does not lack a sense of humor and often confounds the wisdom of the wise. But an erroneous or illusory circumstance will not produce fruits as important, as sustained, as durable, as profound, as an authentic action of God Himself. It is regrettable that more serious efforts are not made to authenticate the fruits of apparitions, for this aspect of discernment, like the others (including the scientific and medical study that examines the psycho-physiological normality of apparitions), calls for patient, laborious and methodical observation.

Even more important than the historical study of apparitions, would be the elaboration of a serious method for discernment, in contrast with the often deplorable methods that currently prevail.

MARY AND APPARITIONS

What is the Blessed Virgin's place in the vast domain of apparitions?

Before considering the quantitative and geographical aspect of this question, it is important to recall that the prototype and foundation for apparitions are those of the risen Christ to the Twelve whom he had chosen as witnesses. They are, according to the Apostle Paul, a prolongation of the Gospel, the very foundation of the faith (*1 Cor.* 15).

His physical victory over the death, inflicted on Him by a sinful world, and which He had assumed, is the fundamental sign, the personal momentous work that gives value to all the others.

Subsequent apparitions, on the other hand, have a humble status in the Church, which discerns them with prudence, watchfulness, and reserve. As much as the Church promotes belief in the Resurrection of the risen Christ, based on the faith of the Apostles, so much does she favor prudence if the risen Christ should reappear today.

This well-grounded difference is complex and difficult to clarify. It is far from being fully elucidated, for, from the psychological point of view, the experience of apparitions does not reveal all the differences that may have been clearly stated.

It is quite difficult to classify the apparition of Christ to St. Paul on the road to Damascus (*Acts* 9:3-9; 22:5-16; 26:9-18). He was not one of the Twelve, but he places this apparition, the last one, on a plane analogous to the others, all the while considering himself as one born out of due time (*1 Cor.* 15:8). He considered himself (and he is considered by the Church) as one of the Twelve, an

Apostle, not as a witness of the life of Christ.

Throughout history, the Church has not been without attaching great value to apparitions. In the seventeenth century, on the eve of rationalism, St. Margaret Mary benefited from this stance with regard to the revelation of the Sacred Heart, a revelation of love, of a Heart misunderstood. The beauty of certain words to her, analogous to those of the Gospel, would merit giving them a high value:

"Behold a heart that has so loved men and that is so little loved."

When all is said and done, there is quite certainly a difference between God's choice and the interpretation of the Church, starting with the first generation. The Resurrection of Christ is a unique and fundamental fact, the final fulfillment of His Incarnation and the eminent sign which His death gave of that Incarnation. The first apparitions are then the foundation for all the rest. Those of Christ later on are given in a way completely relative to these fundamental apparitions, to recall them, to confirm them in the faltering heart of Christians.

Remaining on the psychological plane, we do not have the means to establish the difference between those apparitions (in the course of which the Apostles doubted until they were confirmed by Christ and by the Holy Spirit) and the ones that have followed in the course of centuries with similar characteristics. It would be all the more difficult to establish the difference since we are not in touch with the intimate experience of those who had these initial experiences, and since we cannot perform on the apparitions of Christ the tests that we can perform on apparitions today. That is why it is prudent and reasonable to maintain this theological difference between the apparitions of the risen Christ and the others, humbly aware of the limits of our expertise in this matter. For if we believe in the Resurrection of Christ, it is not because we have greater scientific proofs of it. Even here our proofs on the experimental plane would be very weak. The fundamental importance of these apparitions depends, above all, on the light of God, which is essential to the faith, and whoever neglects to appeal to this freely given light, and to submit himself to it from within, will soon leave the faith which is first of all a gift of God and then an acceptance on the part of man. Although faith is something reasonable and rests on reasons that must be cultivated, the act of faith resembles not so much a scientific proof, such as one works at in a laboratory, as it does the faith by showing confidence in one another, despite their common human frailty. The difference is that faith in God is the most solid foundation because it is supreme Love.

Therefore, compared with the apparitions of Christ, those of the Blessed Virgin remain a secondary phenomenon in the Church, a minor one, whatever may be the social and material importance that they assume.

Furthermore, it is only beginning with the Middle Ages and especially in modern times, since Guadalupe in 1531, and above all since the Miraculous Medal (1830), Lourdes (1858), and Fatima (1917) that they have taken on such a great importance in the life of the Church.

ORIGIN AND DEVELOPMENT

They are not mentioned in the very earliest centuries. The first one attested to is that of Mary to Gregory the Wonderworker, who died around the year 270 (*Gregory of Nyssa,* Life of Gregory the Wonderworker, pg. 46, 909-913 A).

They are more frequent beginning with the sixth century when the account of the apparition to St. Mary of Egypt circulates; in the seventh century with the miracle of Theophilus, freed by the Virgin Mary from his pact with the devil; and in the eighth century with St. John Damascene, to whom the Blessed Virgin is supposed to have restored his hand, cut off by the emir of Damascus.

But these ancient phenomena are hard to verify.

Apparitions have multiplied in the modern era, where they have taken a new direction, as though to meet a new situation: the decay of Christianity, secularization and the progressive materialization of the world.

The first apparition of modern times, at Guadalupe, Mexico, in 1531, came to redirect colonial domination. The Virgin appears not to the Spaniards, but to an Indian, at a site significant to the Indians, that of the cruel goddess Tonantzin. Progressively, the event played a role of considerable importance. According to Jacques Lafaye, professor at the Sorbonne, and other secular historians, it was the birth of a new civilization and of a new culture at the same time as the birth of a new Church in the New World, one that surmounted races and conquest.

Rue du Bac (the Miraculous Medal), Lourdes and Fatima have played analogous roles at key moments of history.

WHY THIS EMINENT PLACE OF MARY?

Why does Mary hold this considerable importance in the sphere of verifiable apparitions?

First of all, her glory, glorified by the Assumption, is visible and can therefore normally manifest itself. This does not mean that in every apparition there is a meeting with the physical body of the Blessed Virgin. On the other hand, there are often visions of the heart, as Jelena of Medjugorje says (interior locutions). More rarely, the apparition is present as a real, exterior person in three dimensions. The seers can touch her; she can embrace them and they retain a profound impression of this.

For all that, in this latter case, perceptible knowledge does not function in the same way as when we see a person in this world facing us. For a long time we have had a first class instance of this. If the body of the Blessed Virgin had descended to the niche in the grotto at Lourdes, the way the body of Christ appeared to the disciples after the Resurrection, everyone would have seen it.

But only Bernadette saw. The communication was made in another way. This conclusion has been confirmed and clarified by medical tests on the seers at Medjugorje and on others.

The frequency of the Blessed Virgin's apparition is also allied to her function as a mother. It is the distinctive feature of a mother to be concerned about her children and to communicate with them, with some kind of permanence. By vocation, Mary shows herself and acts at key moments or in times of grave crisis in history. She came to assist at the birth of the New World at Guadalupe. She comes to visit our media culture in an hour of a crisis, of materialism and multiple moral degradations, calling for special help.

This mission of the Blessed Virgin was prophesied in the Apocalypse. There Mary is described as a glorious sign in the heavens (her Assumption), but in close relation to the earth which she visits. She is shown in her double maternity: with respect to the Messiah (*Rev.* 12:5) and with regard to her "other children," as in *John* 19:25-27. She aids them in spiritual combat.

Is it necessary to link up the current frequency of Marian apparitions to the prophecy of Grignion de Montfort? He believed Mary is called to play a dazzling role in the last days. Like all prophetic views, this one leaves theology to apply the criteria of discernment. Only fulfillment will determine which prophecies are authentic.

CHAPTER 2

Theological Significance

What makes up the unity of this book is that the four topics studied, as diverse as they are, link visible man to God, Who is invisible: the corporal to the spiritual.

They are concerned then with the theology of the image, which establishes the relation of people with God Savior by showing that His transcendance is not an unbridgeable chasm. In fact, according to biblical revelation, God is not the "Totally Other." He made us in His own image and likeness.

What then is an image? It is a reproduction, usually of what is beautiful, for one makes an image only of what is in some way attractive and fascinating. But the image is never an exact double of the object. It only evokes its appearance. It filters and transposes what is most significant.

WHAT IS THE IMAGE OF GOD?

When the Bible speaks of the image of God, it is speaking analogically and poetically, not physically and mathematically. When St. Paul writes: *"The Son is the image of God invisible, the First-born of all creatures,"* the word "image" takes on a special meaning, and in certain respects, one contrary to the pictorial sense, for God does not have a perceptible appearance. *No one has ever seen*

God. (*John* 1:18). The Son is not only similar to, but identical with the Father, exclusive of any perceptible image.

And when man is called the "image" of God, that is merely a transposition of this resemblence into our sensible and bodily realm. It is there that He places His spiritual imprint.

The creation of a spiritual soul animates and transcends our animal body and gives us that which is therefore our very own: a personal consciousness. We are created as persons, automous although created. We receive our liberty as liberty: *"God made him subject to his own free choice,"* says Ben Sira (Sir 15:14).

This "admirable exchange" makes us sacred even in our bodily dimension. Our life then is the fulfillment of the work of salvation in Jesus Christ. Man, being a bodily creature, is not able to bring about his return to God except in a material and bodily, therefore, a perceptible way. Being the image of God, it is through a world of signifying and significant images that we make our way toward God: the image being the mediatory stage in our participation in God. Since we are essentially corporal, it is with both body and soul that we advance towards God.

FOUR PRIVILEGED EXAMPLES OF THE IMAGE

It is within the orbit of this plan of God, and this theology of the image, that the four phenomena studied in the book find their meaning.

1. The pilgrimage is a significant expression of our impulsion towards God. It involves our body with our soul, through space and time, on a journey and towards an end. It symbolizes that our whole life is a journey towards God and also causes this wayfaring relationship to advance.

2. The sanctuary, a holy place consecrated to God (which is the goal of the pilgrimage), is on the contrary a static image. It is also the sacred space of an encounter, a protective shelter and one hallowed by personal and liturgical prayer. But a church of stone is only an image

and a repository for the Church, the mystical body of Christ. This mediatory sign leads to and fosters the reciprocal habitation of God and man, which Jesus teaches tirelessly in the fourth Gospel:

"Live in me and I in you, as I live in the Father and the Father in me." (*John* 6:56). This is a major theme of the New Testament.

3. The icon precipitates contemplation, which is, according to St. Thomas Aquinas, the very definition of holiness. It offers to our sight not only the image of the divine world, the heavenly Jerusalem, of those who dwell in the realm of God, but the gaze of that world and of God Himself upon us. Thus icons, born of prayer and fasting in the eastern tradition, bring about the birth of prayer, asceticism and charity, whereby man detaches himself from himself, in order to go towards God alone, where he will find everything else.

4. Authentic apparitions and visions are not man-made works like icons. They arise from life itself; where they are authentic, they proceed from a movement of God, not through an ascent of man towards God. All the same, this communication is not something purely passive on the part of the seer, whose receptivity is active. Not only does the seer receive the interior image according to his or her own capacity and sensitivity, but is involved in this perception where the essential is the very light of God.

Of the four signs studied, the principal one is the sanctuary, the dwelling of God, dwelling with God, Who wishes to be All in All. He brings about this transforming inhabitation by means of the Eucharist (a symbolic and real image). It substantially brings about in life itself the presence prefigured by the sacred object that was the Ark of the Covenant. While the church building is only a sign of the Church as mystical body, the true dwelling of Christ, it is also the place for the liturgy, where God reveals Himself objectively to every believing subject. This is why Jesus loved *"the house of his Father"* (*Luke* 2:48

and *John* 2:17).

These signs, which are held in honor and in popular piety, belong to the religious dimension of Christianity. Following the lead of some Protestant theologians, a number of conciliar theologians, after Vatican II, advocated a faith without religion. At the end of the 60's, Harvey Cox, in his *The Secular City*, had radically prophesied the end of all liturgy, in favor of social action alone. But, beginning in 1973, he became the apologist and prophet of the feast, of liturgy, of popular religion, even Catholic religion. (*The Seduction of the Spirit, the Use and Misuse of People's Religion*, New York, 1973). At the same time, he discovered the Virgin Mary. In this book (p. 177) he wrote paradoxically, *"If God is dead, Mary is alive and very much alive,"* while Theodore Rozak, the prophet of the counter culture wrote in his turn:

"How poor and unbalanced is a religion that finds no place for the divine Mother" (*Where the Wasteland Ends,* Doubleday, 1972, p. 133).

If Christianity is essentially faith in God, it is, more specifically, faith in God incarnated to save mankind: God entered into human solidarity, concrete and perceptible, and this involves a religion. The word comes from the Latin *religare*: to bind, signifying concrete and perceptible bonds. These bonds are not abstract. They imply body and image, like family values, since it (religion) makes us enter the family of God.

Popular values, pilgrimages, sanctuaries, icons and apparitions are authentically Catholic, because they are authentically Christian.

Mary, the sole human author of the Incarnation, and one who took part in popular religion, holds a key position in this domain, on a theological, typological and pastoral level. She contemplated the image of God in the body formed within her, for the Word of God: the perfect image of the Father.

THE
RIEHLE
FOUNDATION...

The Riehle Foundation is a non-profit, tax-exempt, charitable organization that exists to produce and/or distribute Catholic material to anyone, anywhere.

The Foundation is dedicated to the Mother of God and her role in the salvation of mankind. We believe that this role has not diminished in our time, but, on the contrary has become all the more apparent in this the era of Mary as recognized by Pope John Paul II, whom we strongly support.

During the past four years the foundation has distributed books, films, rosaries, bibles, etc. to individuals, parishes, and organizations all over the world. Additionally, the foundation sends materials to missions and parishes in a dozen foreign countries.

Donations forwarded to The Riehle Foundation for the materials distributed provide our sole support. We appreciate your assistance, and request your prayers.

IN THE SERVICE OF JESUS AND MARY
All for the honor and glory of God!

The Riehle Foundation
P.O. Box 7
Milford, OH 45150